DAY TRADE LIKE A MILLIONAIRE

DAY TRADE LIKE A MILLIONAIRE

No More Trading Multiple Strategies, Tickers,
Technical Indicators, or Fundamental Analysis

MAURICE KENNY

CONTENTS

BEFORE YOU CONTINUE READING

As my gift to you, here's access to my free one-hour webinar that will teach you my strategy that I use for day trading.

Don't have time to read the book? Scan the QR code below or go to the URL to learn about my strategy.

 Use your phone's camera to scan the QR code
OR
https://mauricekenny790.lpages.co/webinar-intro/

Meet Maurice Kenny

Until I learned trading well enough to earn a living, Christmastime and New Years produced nightmares and annually freaked me out, nearly to the point of post-traumatic stress. Have you ever seen everyone around Christmas smiling, happy, and laughing, but you just had to be the only person in a 1000-mile radius that just got the worst news ever? Being kicked to the curb or hearing corporate speak of "we're re-aligning our priorities with a new strategic vision so as a result your role is no longer needed, but we sure appreciate your hard work and dedication" during the happiest time of the year is the worst.

I was an information technology manager at a Fortune 500 company, a damn good one—director level at multiple stops—but I couldn't survive the holidays, <u>FOUR consecutive years!</u> The final red card I returned to my office, closed the door, sat down and sobbed crocodile tears, "What's wrong with me!?! All I want is to help people in this company."

That last Christmas letting-go stabbed most because Kim and I were preparing to get married AND buy our first home. We were in the final days before settlement and worried sick the loan approval would be rescinded. Somehow we managed to close and pay for our wedding, I began receiving unemployment and liquidated my $22,000 401k as we plugged the dam pooling our savings and cutting unnecessary purchases. Our monthly expenses totaled $3,500 for mortgage and basic bills; quick math shows how solvent we were. I had to find another job pronto.

That's when some combination of divine intervention, coincidence and good luck shepherded me toward my first trade. Within the same week but during separate conversations with two people I respect, my father-in-law and brother-in-law, each encouraged me to consider day trading; they said that's where the money is if I could figure out and felt I'd be well suited since I'm analytical. So I plunged down the rabbit hole by Googling, "How to day trade".

My brain awash in information, I pushed myself off the deep end trading real money without paper trading. Since I wasn't sure which of the gazillion indicators or strategies might work, I sampled as many as possible to find something that stuck. I loaded my charts with a spaghetti mess of colored lines. I tried penny stocks because they're cheap and move quickly. I read the financial news, watched shows and videos and tried trading off fundamentals.

And lo and behold, I flushed $5,000 my first month! Back to the lab again, next I typed into the Google Machine, "How to make $5,000 day trading" to recoup my loss. After flooding my brain with even more data, I reloaded my dual monitors with a DOZEN indicators and also traded that many stocks. Then it happened, I lost ANOTHER $5,000 and eventually chewed through my retirement savings, the one thing I now preach NOBODY should risk.

I felt lonely flailing at the bottom, but I genuinely enjoy trading so I didn't give up. I also understand the definition of lunacy is repeating the same behaviors expecting different results. So what had to go?

I noticed among the dozen tickers I watched they bounced off basic lines of support and resistance, so why did I need the clutter of all the lagging indicators showing me price action I could plainly see? I also missed trades because I was following too many stocks among the graphical noise, so I began eliminating tickers as well.

I went from a dozen to ten, then eight, and finally only Microsoft (MSFT) and the SPDR S&P 500 ETF Trust (SPY). One session in particular I watched MSFT on the right screen and SPY on the left; the Microsoft trade failed but SPY worked. So I said, "Screw it", I'm going to focus only on SPY and I no longer care about the others.

I began winning but observed the SPY candlesticks didn't always tap the primary resistance lines, they came close but didn't exactly touch again. I saw other traders drew deeper support and resistance, buffer areas the candle bodies or wicks reached repeatedly, but I couldn't figure out why their zones were necessarily the depth they were, so I feverishly back-tested over months during different years of SPY trading sessions and observed the zone depth was generally around ten cents in stock price give or take pennies.

Being a fan of simplicity, I applied 10-cent, taller resistance and support zones onto my charts and viola!, progress, I began consistently winning half my trades. Finally, I developed the specific entry and exit criteria I'll teach you and started winning up to 90 percent of my trades!

During a full month, I made $500 a day and remember thinking, "I just made $10,000 in one month, I might be onto something!" So I wrote down my procedure, focused only on trading SPY using but a single indicator and maintained a consistent winning percentage between 70-90 percent (i.e. I won between seven and nine of every ten trades). And the best part, I got back my time and life!

At this point I had day-traded for a full year, built complete confidence in my system and banked great coin; but, because I rely on preset zone alerts and only make a trade or two daily (and sometimes none if the chart doesn't inform me), I had a lot of time to fill and only so many movies to watch.

I began clicking around Facebook, helping others for free because I had nothing better to do. One friend, LaShana, asked for my guidance privately so I began tutoring her over the phone. Around six weeks later, she called crying, "Because of you I finally make enough money to work part-time and can now be at home with my kids watching my babies grow up!" That's why I teach, and have chased that high ever since by coaching hundreds of people from around the world!

I wish that for YOU, to have the life you want however you decide. "Work" is nothing but trading your time and skills for a wage. My layoffs jeopardized my family and baked into my brain that I truly didn't have control over my future no matter how hard or well I performed within the company org chart. I had no idea I could work for myself and potentially make unlimited income trading on my own time. You deserve FREEDOM too!

Our roadmap begins on the next page with the Agenda.

Agenda

I won't bore you with irrelevant background about the markets nor promote magical indicators and scanners. I teach everything I learned the hard way, so you don't have to!

You're reading this likely because you are either brand new to trading or you struggled with other strategies. You're far from alone. **Ninety percent of traders FAIL** and I promise I will teach you to the best of my ability how the leading 10 percent earn a living so you can join us.

While succinct, I share a lot of information; therefore, you will most effectively absorb the system by reading the concepts step-by-step, putting down the book and practicing implementing them, first by paper trading, then later using real money with only one contract to start.

Do NOT use retirement savings and only risk an amount you are comfortable losing. Past performance is a promise of NOTHING and the success/failure of others doesn't impact your bank account aside from what you learn from them.

I add continually to our educational website so please regularly visit MauriceKennyTrading.com for free teaching lessons, tools, resources and videos. All of this information works together. If you prefer one-on-one attention, consider joining our coaching program at MauriceKenny.com. And don't forget our social channels, especially YouTube (Maurice Kenny).

Let's begin.

#1 Introduction to Options: How do Hedge Funds Trade?

I should more accurately entitle: "How Smart Money takes your's!" Why care about what hedge fund managers and other market makers do? Because we're going to copy them on a smaller scale, ride their coattails, that's the secret to becoming a Top Ten Percent trader by emulating Big Money.

#2 Anticipate Stock Movement: Supply and Demand Zone Trading Strategy

This core strategy provides our bread and butter and is, if not THE single, certainly among the simplest trading strategies if you maintain discipline and don't overcomplicate by gumming up your charts with multiple indicators and mixing in other strategies. If like me you're a fan of the KISS Method (Keep it super simple), you're going to love this approach.

#3 Trade like a Sniper

Profitable trading distills to emotionless entries and exits, which depends predominantly on your mindset reading what the chart informs. We don't chase trades, we allow price action to alert us when and how to enter and exit. No guessing, we allow the chart to tell its story and follow our plan, every single time.

#4 How to Properly LOSE Money

What!?! (Did he just write that?) <u>Accept that you are going to lose</u>, we all do, but I'll teach you the correct way to set your stop losses, whether to use automated or mental stops, and even how to handle losing streaks. Remember to trade like a sniper, eliminate emotions and reconcile you WILL lose, it's just a matter of moving on after losing properly.

One Last Thing: Think or Swim (TOS)

I'm referring to the trading platform I recommend but you may be thinking sink or swim as you begin. As we start, just take the lessons one baby step at a time, don't try to eat the elephant in one bite, a marathon begins with a single step.

You're free to use whichever trading platform you prefer but I strongly recommend thinkorswim®, specifically the desktop version, which I explain in a video at MauriceKenneyTrading.com.

Proceed setting up TOS (pronounced "toss") so that you can begin practicing as you progress through this book. Continually practicing with pretend money is paramount to becoming comfortable developing this new skill. You will practice even after you begin trading real money and should practice daily to fast track your experience.

Finally, remember the Supply and Demand Strategy is foremost risk and self management, trading comes second. Our goal, **keep it simple and let the trades come to us**.

To your success, and we're off!

1

About YOU!

I shared my background, now your turn. Either on your device or paper, I want you to physically answer the following questions by either typing or writing. You will think about as well but there's a neurobiological, brain benefit to physically "writing" the responses.

Plus if you're serious about making trading a career, assessing your current circumstance is Step 1 planning strategically.

1. **Why trade (core reason, your WHY)?**
2. **What are your financial goals?**
3. **What is your current win ratio?**
4. **What is your trading strategy and process?**
5. **What are your trading strengths and weaknesses?**

If you're brand new, mark NA (non-applicable) for those questions beyond the first two, but begin mulling over as you read through this text, by the end you will have answered each in detail.

As you contemplate, I'll answer each to model for you. At the end of this chapter, stop reading, thoroughly think through and write down your answers to compare later once you've completed this book.

Number 1: *WHY do I trade?*

As you just read, I was laid off multiple times and forced to find a new way to earn income. But I could've stayed in the same industry, or easily transferred my skills to any number of other companies outside corporate America. So why day trading, which seems crazy risky to the uninformed?

Drilling down, I wanted freedom from employers, to be self-reliant providing for my family. I didn't want another person determining— more accurately undermining—my job and income. I couldn't continue working under the annual threat of lay-offs, especially during the holidays, and had to prioritize my family's life. <u>I needed self-determination</u>.

So given all of your skills and attributes, and beyond money, why trade?

<u>Keep asking yourself "why" until you feel your answer is exactly right in your heart, not just your head</u>. Later in this text I provide a guided exercise for you to drill down to your ultimate why.

Number 2: *How much money do you need and/or want?*

Break this down into six-month, one-year and long term goals.

What's the monthly minimum you need to not feel like you're struggling?

That bottom line, income threshold is defined as paying all of your bills with enough left over for saving in a rainy day fund for unexpected urgencies or emergencies (e.g. vehicle repairs, medical co-pays). If you save a certain amount for retirement, give to charity, donate to school or tithe to church, count those as "bills" for this calculation.

What's that total with a little left over monthly so you're not losing sleep?

Next, what do you aspire to make annually considering other "nice-to-haves", like vacations or other discretionary expenses you may have been deferring (e.g. trips, home improvement, indulgent splurges)?

And if everything goes according to plan, what are your financial needs longer term including college expenses and your ideal retirement?

For me, I had to bring home $3,500 monthly ($42,000 annually) to cover our basic cost of living. My medium goal was six-figures annually in order to live comfortably. Now that I've achieved those, my long term financial goal has shifted to building my business from a specific strategic mission: I want our program to develop 100, six-figure-earning, day traders.

<u>What is your dream income?</u>

Calculate based on your requirements and these factors:

252 trading days per year:

$200/day = $50,400/year
$400/day = $100,800/year
$1,000/day =$252,000/year
$4,000/day = $1,048,000/year

Number 3: *How often do you win (percentage)?*

<u>Divide your Wins by Total Trades</u>. If you've won eight out of ten trades (8 ÷ 10 = 0.80 or 80 percent). Five out of ten is 50 percent. If you're a beginner, start tracking from your first simulated, "paper" trade.

I maintain an 80 percent winning percentage, trading five days and typically winning four of my five weekly trades.

You might be thinking, "You only execute five trades a week!?!" Generally yes, because I'm trading 100 contracts per trade, so the amount at risk and won is magnified. If I win, I shut off the computer, same when I lose. The wins and losses are much bigger at 100 contracts.

You'll start with one contract and develop consistency before moving up; but, your ultimate goal is 20-100 contracts based on the funds you have to risk, the type of trade you are considering (e.g. Power Hour volatility), and whether you're trading full-time or as a side hustle.

Key point I'll reiterate throughout, **being a "day trader" doesn't mean you MUST trade ALL day.** We seek quality, not quantity. If I'm trading 20 days a month, I don't want to lose more than four, and I don't trade every day. I only buy when the chart tells me, I don't force trades.

If you know that you're only going to potentially make ONE trade a session, that forces you to be patiently picky, which mitigates mental challenges we all face that I'll describe later, such as fear of missing out (FOMO), chasing candles, over-trading, greed, fear, frustration, perfectionism, overconfidence, elation, etc.

The win percentage measures your discipline sticking to the rules, your bank account (profit and loss) demonstrates your monetary success. And this might blow your mind, but you can have a negative day on the P&L but succeed in following your plan, so that's a good day!

Number 4: *What is your trading system (strategy, tactics, process, rules)?*

Cold water in your face, if you can't answer right this minute with specifics, then arbitrariness and happenstance are ruling your trading and that's likely why you're struggling. In other words, if you don't have a system, then NO System is YOUR system and you're randomly guessing with your money (i.e. speculating, gambling).

Good news! I'm going to teach you a proven method that will consistently produce results so long as you remain <u>disciplined</u>. My core strategy follows Japanese candlesticks reacting to supply and demand zones of support and resistance you will learn to recognize, draw on your charts and execute trades when, and only when, price action informs you to buy and sell. No more guessing or trading on whims.

You will become sniper focused and emotionless. I will teach you how to manage yourself as you keep an eye on only ONE indicator while being mindful of trading volume. We will keep things SIMPLE, and above all DISCIPLINED, until your trading becomes second nature. Avoid being a jack of all trades and master of none.

Number 5: *What are your trading strengths and weaknesses?*

From this day forward in your trading lifetime, you will continually assess and track your strengths and weaknesses so that you're aware of how your emotional state affects your profit and loss. We each have strong and weak points, which change with overall experience and even time of day. Managing yourself is ninety percent of the trading game. I devote **Chapter 9** to the mental and emotional hurdles, so begin monitoring yours now, even during practice trades.

My trading strength is also my weakness because I follow my supply and demand zone system EXACTLY, and I only trade one ticker (SPY), which means I miss opportunities because I don't follow anything else. I even miss SPY plays because I don't stare at my monitors all day, chase nor guess; I don't enter a trade until the chart slaps me awake and I typically only execute a single trade a session, if that.

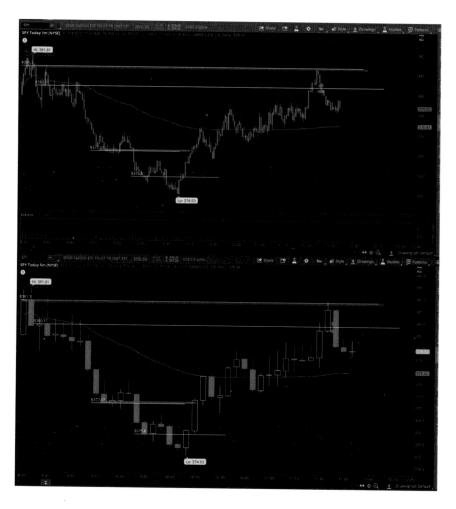

So yes, I leave money on the table but I'm disciplined (you're going to read and hear that word a lot) about maintaining for myself no less than a 80 percent winning percentage, and the minimum benchmark for everyone is 70 percent. I detest losing so I developed a system that produces like a machine if you stick to the plan and remain.......? You got this.

2

Who are the Market Makers?

Let's define the competition and playing field so you understand the rationale supporting the strategy and tactics.

I am not describing the traditional market of buy and hold investors saving for retirement who contribute to their accounts on schedule or with variable installments. Our daily trading arena is made up of two primary groups, Big Money and retail traders like us, the Jack's and Jill's. The entire market is just individual people but our side cannot defeat Big Money because we don't have the same resources (e.g. huge capital positions, automated algorithms, microsecond order fulfillment, etc); but we can mimic, and they actually need us in a symbiotic relationship.

Who is Big Money? They are institutional insiders, the market makers, which is how I'll refer to them henceforth. Also known as Smart Money, market makers can literally move market prices due to their huge position sizes and liquidity; they are hedge funds, mutual funds, institutional investors, large banks, insurance companies, any entity maintaining and investing the assets of others, including the buy and hold, retirement investors.

Money never rests and you can bet it's ALL about maximizing returns. The market makers practice arbitrage, borrowing at a lower rate and earning a higher rate, in tandem with buying low and selling high. Rest assured they make money whether the market is going up, down or sideways because, per literal definition of hedging, they're playing all sides at once to "hedge their bets".

The market makers employ vast stores of capital from their investors as well as cutting edge systems (e.g. programmed, high frequency trading platforms), which enables them to establish prices in any asset classes in which they choose to participate, and they're also competing against each other. Think of them as product wholesalers, who buy at cost and sell at retail, thereby earning profit and generating even more capital (compounding liquidity) to replenish their "asset warehouse" and perpetuate positive cash flow.

So why do they need little ole us?

Because they take our money! Retail traders serve as fodder, another source of capital. They milk us, and their positions are so ginormous, they need the little guy as a counterbalance in order to actually affect pricing the way they target. The vast majority of retail day traders lose and Smart Money vacuums up that cash from mining stop losses, which they can see. So Smart Money needs us and we cannot beat them, but we can ride their coattails, which is the basis of my Supply and Demand Zone trading strategy.

In fact, we ONLY buy when the market makers tell us. How do we know? By watching the price action of the candlestick patterns forming and reacting to our supply and demand zones relative to trading volume, which is the telling signal. The market makers cannot hide from volume indicators because their positions are so huge, like hiding an elephant behind a beach towel. Large volume tips their hand and we learn to read the resultant chart patterns to assess when to buy and sell.

We follow strict rules so that we trade WITH the market makers and not against. **Remember always, the trend is our friend**. When Smart Money is buying, I am too and vice versa. They have tools and assets we don't, so why fight it? If they're making $2M on a single play, how does $2,000, $200 or $20 per option contract sound to you? There's nothing wrong with being a small fish in a big pond as long as you mimic the big fish and avoid getting eaten, otherwise known as blowing up your account.

The great equalizer, volatility affects all players in the market, even Smart Money. During the pandemic, the ranks of retail traders swelled, which meant even more losers since the majority of Jack's and Jill's trade on gut instinct, therefore the market waters became muddier. Imagine how unpredictable the market gets when there are so many competing interests transacting in milliseconds.

Volatility is why my Supply and Demand Strategy is both easy to understand and implement, but also challenging to master because you will battle your emotions and must be disciplined throughout the chop of cross currents.

Good news, our system is eighth grade simple, but that will tantalize you into over complicating. Listen to me now and believe later, you will stray from the basics by adding "just one more" indicator, price line or trading tool because only trading major supply and demand zones is so simple you fall into the trap of believing adding another thing can't possibly hurt. Clutter is our enemy, keep price action super simple (KISS).

I conclude this chapter with a few foundational truths about day trading you have experienced, or will soon, before we dive into the nuts and bolts of the Supply and Demand Strategy:

- The more retail traders in the arena, the more losers and increased market volatility.
- The majority of traders don't have a mentor nor a procedure they follow every trade.
- No plan or mentor means by default the Market becomes your teacher.
- Everyone loses.
- Without a strategic and tactical edge, you will lose more often.
- Each loss costs money, compounded if you're trading multiple contracts.

Next I teach how to mimic the market makers and trade WITH the market. We'll go with the flow, never against the current, practicing PATIENCE awaiting confirmation to enter and exit our trades based only on what the price action informs.

3

Demystifying the Hedger's Strategy

Now that you understand the players in the field, let's delve into what they're doing and the flow of money as the basis for the Supply and Demand Zones you'll be drawing on your five-minute charts. Once you recognize within the context of volume and volatility, planning whether to buy or sell will be clearer because you will understand why you're seeing, for example, quick/large chart movements or long/short/wicky candles forming. With experience you'll know whether to sit on the sidelines or take a trade based on how the chart is forming.

First, a stock is born. A company wishes to raise capital by issuing shares, and engages an investment bank to structure an Initial Public Offering (IPO) at a price the bank and company agree properly values the stock. Those new shares come at the best, "preferred" price, as well as top debt priority, than what retail traders can purchase later, which is common stock. After the original offering, the market dictates through open trading the company's eventual value by its price per share, but think of the IPO price as what would be the wholesale cost for a physical product.

The hedge funds get first crack at the preferred shares at the best price and begin buying and selling, which immediately alters the original offered price they received, and we haven't yet seen. Finally, last in line, Joe Public, the retail trader, gets our chance to buy common shares after a middle man, the broker dealer, offers through an exchange. Everyone along the chain is getting a cut with the cost worked into the revenue. For example, the preferred share price might've been $10 at IPO and now, with hats in hand, the retail trader gets our chance to buy at $15 with the market in motion. We're last in line for everything, including repayment should any scraps be left after a corporate bankruptcy.

The hedge funds receive money to invest from clients and their primary mission is cash flow (liquidity), keeping the money moving and continuously earning in every direction so they get more for their clients and themselves. Here's where the literal market maker comes into play, a person or department, they strategize a target price and use the capital assets at their disposal to move or "make" the market. They "hedge", even against themselves, by buying and selling to affect the price, covering all sides of their bets, so that each position makes money no matter what. You've heard, "Heads I win, tails you lose?", that's them. But that doesn't mean we can't be friends!

Remember they have information systems and tools to manipulate prices due to their huge positions and microsecond, execution speed. They're competing against each other and also dealing with us, the little fish clogging their pond. And that's why you see the candlesticks and resultant chart patterns forming and moving as it does. The market makers are battling each other and all of us retail traders swirling in the mix, which is why some days are more volatile than others (e.g. Fridays, sessions leading into holidays, Federal Reserve meeting days).

With experience you'll be able to spot what they're doing based on how the candles form and move because, while we don't have the same resources, volume is daylight, gives away Smart Money's moves and we can mirror them. You'll be able to spot and adjust your trading intentions accordingly within the parameters of the Supply and Demand Strategy.

Now before proceeding, if you'd like to see market makers in action without knowing anything technical, log into your trading platform and watch the first few, one-minute candlesticks forming at opening bell and last minutes of each trading day. The final sixty minutes, called Power Hour, is volatile most sessions but particularly the last three minutes when the power brokers move large positions seconds before closing bell.

Sit back and watch the candlesticks surge and plummet, often alternating colors in huge moves within milliseconds, faster than you can click your mouse button. Those are the market makers battling each other with many poorly positioned and guessing, retail traders caught in the torrent. Don't let that be you!

4

How You target Supply and Demand Zones

We've arrived at the core strategy, a simplified version of what the market makers do that we will mimic. I've explained the who, what, when and why of the macro market; now we dive into the micro tactics and how we'll enter the battle as retail, options traders, the small fry in the day trading ocean.

Supply and demand is the equilibrium between the price and volume of shares traded. Any imbalance is profitable, which is what the market makers create and where we trade riding their coattails.

Green candles are buyers (Bulls), red candles are sellers (Bears). We draw on our charts the Supply and Demand Zones visually representing the agreement in price between buyers and sellers at a specific time, then patiently wait for price friction to develop at the areas we've identified where and when we can profit.

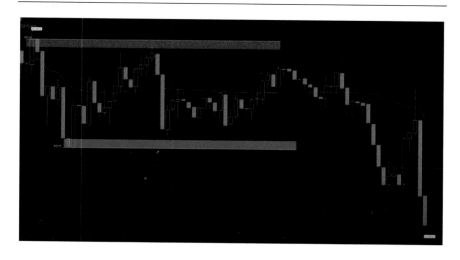

The zones are rectangles, ten cents in depth, established <u>during the first hour of trading</u> (9:30 - 10:30 EST). The very top and bottom zones are **Major Zones (MZ)**. We delineate the top most, major zone as the **Major Supply Zone (MSZ)** and its bottom counterpart as the **Major Demand Zone (MDZ)**. The supply zone rectangles are red, the demand zone blocks green. Simply, the highest red zone the first hour is major supply, the lowest green zone is major demand.

We wait until 10:30 EST to draw the major zones to allow the session to get under away and let the trading waters settle. The first and last hour are typically the most volatile with increased volume, often huge, rapid moves. The first half hour is influenced most by market makers positioning and also premarket levels, activity begins to even out closer to 10:30 EST when we will have a clearer, calmer view of that day's newest zones, which is why we wait instead of jumping right into the mayhem at opening bell.

Learn how to recognize and physically draw the major zones within your trading platform by watching my free webinar at MauriceKenney.com. Now is the ideal time for you to do this so you can begin practicing as you complete this text.

What do the major zones represent?

The **Major Demand Zone (MDZ) is the lowest** price line **PLUS-10 cents**. The **Major Supply Zone (MSZ)** is the **highest** price line **MINUS-10 cents**. For ease of writing repeatedly, I'm going to use the abbreviations MSZ for major supply and MSD for major demand zones.

Once delineated, the MDZ and MSZ remain on the chart the entire session as "majors", even though others might form and replace them as trading progresses. <u>Remember, the first major zones of the session always remain "major" and influential the rest of the day.</u>

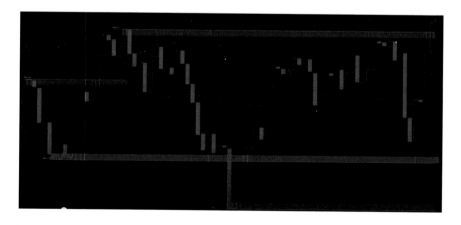

If/when either major zone is violated AFTER the first hour, then the most recent high and low become the newest MDZ and MSZ respectively, otherwise the major zones from the first hour remain throughout the day and anything else that forms similarly in between is a Minor Zone. Even when replaced by newer supply and demand zones, we still pay attention to the original major zones of the session because they still pack punch as respected areas of resistance and support, but the newest, top and bottom majors usurp them as our primary trading targets.

For the purposes of written instruction only, without a corresponding graphic so you understand the math, lets say a SPY option is trading low within the first hour at 300, the green and red candles agree that's the price at a given time, so you draw a price line at 300.00, then add the rectangle from among the drawing options tools and create the Major Demand Zone (MDZ) PLUS ten cents atop that line, at 300.10 at the bottom of your chart.

Your Major Supply Zone (MSZ) within the session's first hour would be the opposite, above at the top of the chart, the highest point <u>where the candles agree</u> on the price for this same SPY option. Let's say for example, 305.50, so that's where you would draw your price line and then create the zone rectangle starting ten cents below that line (minus 10) to 305.40. I will show graphical examples but want you to focus on the zone cushion math for now, which is simply plus- or minus-ten onto the priceline of agreement.

Let's pause to describe in more detail and give examples of what these zones represent because I don't want you confusing with generic lines of support and resistance. Major zones do act as lines of support and resistance but way more is happening, which you must understand to properly assess. Each individual candle and grouping of candles is also instructive, which I explain later.

Besides resistance and support, what do these zones tell us?

On the low side, the MDZ is informing that buyers and sellers agree this is as low as the price will go for that option contract at that time, sellers aren't willing to sell nor buyers willing to purchase below that zone during that point in the session and perhaps all day if the zone holds. The MSZ is simply the opposite, buyers won't purchase at a higher price, the sellers are topped out at that point, the market is saying the option isn't worth more. This hints at where things might be headed based on the resulting price action and candle patterns.

At the moment this happens, we're at equilibrium, a green and red candle agree, but not for long, as in milliseconds not for long. Three things can happen, the price is rejected to the upside, to a higher price, or to the downside to a lower price, or sideways action (consolidation) until it definitively breaks one way or the other during a tug of war among all traders. The market makers and everyone reacting will decide.

At this point, you might be wondering how this is any different than basic lines of support and resistance and why I created the ten-cent buffer for each major zone.

Imagine the zones as a battlefield where the bulls and bears are working out the next price. When I was losing trades by getting in too soon, out too late, or missing trades entirely, I relied on traditional lines of support/resistance and lagging indicators (i.e. old news).

I became frustrated the many times the candles wouldn't cooperate, got ever so close, but the train left the station without me! They would either just miss the lines, or run through by just a little but not to the same point repeatedly. That's when I took timeout to go into trade simulation and began backtesting over years and different months, tracking hundreds of paper trades, and discovered these areas I labeled as major zones—which is just what I call them, you won't see that anywhere else.

My analysis showed there was and is roughly a ten cent buffer that was respected <u>the majority of the time give or take a few cents.</u> I want to be clear nobody can predict the direction of the market, past performance doesn't promise the future. However, the zones do provide an edge in assessing price action, an educated guess is better than the WAG Method (wild arbitrary guessing), especially when also considering the overall trend, volume and the individual candles and patterns forming. Trading ONLY major zones instead of every line of support and resistance mitigates totally flying blind, guessing when to jump in or out, or trading on gut instinct. Patience, discipline and experience will become your guideposts.

Major KISS Zones

Not what some of you are thinking!

Instead, **KEEP IT SUPER SIMPLE** drawing your major zones. I do. Many of my graduates are stunned to learn their leader ends each trading day with only two major zones on his chart, because I delete the former MZs as they are replaced. Why keep the clutter? As a beginner, you should only be trading MZs, but even advanced traders benefit from "less is more" clarity, so clean up your chart as the session progresses.

The major zones represent the market makers moving price and the insider's automated robots only do that a few times daily for liquidity. At the end of the trading day, your chart should typically show a minimum of two and maybe a total of six, major zones formed throughout the session, with more than half a dozen atypical and possibly a red flag you are over analyzing. If you've got more than six MAJOR zones, then the market is either rocketing skyward, repeatedly establishing new highs, or falling off a cliff to lower lows; you're probably overthinking if that's not the case, so fewer lines the better. But remember, <u>at any one time during trading, there can be only ONE of each major zone</u>, so don't visually bog down your brain.

Granted, it gets a little more complicated when a single, major zone transitions from Supply to Demand and vice versa in the same session. And there are minor zones, which can act like a major if retested multiple times throughout the day, despite not technically being a major zone (i.e. not at the very top and bottom of the chart), but I don't congest my chart drawing them. Later I will cover these more advanced scenarios.

But if you never learned about minor zones and focused only on majors, you will succeed by sticking to the basics.

Pickiness Pays!

This is an ideal time to reemphasize keeping it simple, remaining patient and picky. If and when you get too far into the weeds adding lines and zones, stop, lean back, examine your chart and reorient on just the major zones, the highest and lowest areas where the candles agree. <u>Your beginner's challenge is to maintain discipline, recognize, draw and ONLY trade the major zones</u>. That's it.

"That's it!?!"

I wish I had a dollar for each one of you thinking that right now. The vast majority of you will start out fine while learning (i.e. "That won't be me!") because you don't know better, but then once comfortable with the basics, fall into the trap of overcomplicating the strategy.

I've got a lot more to teach you but want to pause and reiterate the top failing, or more accurately flailing, the coaches and I see repeatedly are new supply and demand traders <u>losing discipline and not keeping the system simple</u>. Ask the other students. First symptom, you begin adding lines and cluttering your charts, soon thereafter you can't see the major zone forest through all the line trees.

Properly implemented, you will draw your major zones after the first hour, set price level alarms just above your MDZ and beneath your MSZ, then stop staring at your monitor and work on something else (or practice trade) until those alerts are triggered. At first, waiting will feel like torture and you will worry you are missing trades, but <u>trust the process and resist the FOMO (Fear of Missing Out) enemy</u>.

Once the price tests your major zone, you will decide whether to enter a trade based on assessing multiple confirmations, volume and by following exact entry criteria I'm about to cover.

You will only enter a trade after:

- Establishing stop loss and take profit areas.
- Deciding the amount of wiggle room to give the trade if price action reverses (i.e. the trend rarely heads all up or down at once)
- Noticing volume levels
- Accepting the risk you are about to undertake (i.e. be OK with losing).

All this preplanning occurs before you click the buy button. Your mental mindset will rule your move and assessing risk will guide you. We manage ourselves and risks first, and trade second.

At the risk of beating into the ground, ask yourself, why would anyone want to overcomplicate this? The more frequently you trade, the greater statistical probability you might lose.

You probably arrived here after trying other complex strategies. Would you rather make thousands of dollars off ONE, daily trade lasting minutes, or stare at your screen for hours, obsessing over and drawing numerous minor zones and placing a half dozen potentially losing trades? Can you be right for three to five minutes?

We seek quality over quantity. I'd rather wait forever and win than rush and lose. We want the stock to prove it's worth trading and never chase. This strategy ideally becomes so second nature it's BORING, and you become PICKY entering ONE or possibly TWO highly profitable trades daily, then call it a day and enjoy your FREEDOM.

Next, confirming your entries, exits and calmly pulling the trigger like a sniper.

BEFORE YOU CONTINUE READING

As my gift to you, here's access to my free one-hour webinar that will teach you my strategy that I use for day trading.

Don't have time to read the book? Scan the QR code below or go to the URL to learn about my strategy.

Use your phone's camera to scan the QR code
OR
https://mauricekenny790.lpages.co/webinar-intro/

5

Your Favorite Letters: ZRCE

For my next trick, I'll make your head spin by covering an alphabet soup of must-know acronyms, but I promise you'll grow fond of one.

We trade a single ticker symbol: **SPY, the SPDR S&P 500 ETF Trust**. ETF is for Electronically Traded Fund; ETFs trade like individual stocks and afford a level of inflation protection by enabling you to sell quickly.

Why only SPY?

SPY represents the entire S&P market index of the 500 most capitalized companies, spread across different sectors, which provides diversification because you're getting a sliver of each humongous company among multiple well monetized industries. Every stock has a personality and, by focusing on the entire market, we're avoiding the pitfalls of individual company news, earnings, events, scandals, CEO/owner quirks, hostile takeovers, mergers, bankruptcies, stock splits, etc.

Furthermore, we don't buy individual shares, which are too expensive for day trading unless you have beaucoup bucks. We rely on the power of leverage to increase our buying power purchasing stock **option contracts, not the actual company shares**— one option includes 100 shares of its underlying asset at a lower price premium.

A single share of Tesla (TSLA) might cost $700, whereas its corresponding option includes 100 shares for hundreds less because you are getting a contract to purchase that many shares and not actually receiving the shares (i.e. the contract is an "option" to buy/sell shares with all the rights as if you already own).

Options 101: The bare basics

Options are tradable financial instruments, contracts, which give the buyer the right to buy and sell call and put options for an underlying asset, in our case the SPY ETF.

Remember the difference between calls and puts with this memory aid, you "call up" and "put down". So if you think the market is going up, you buy a call option, and when you feel the market will retreat, you buy a put option. You sell each when you want to take profit or cut a loss.

Options come in different time frames before the contract "expires". Options expire worthless and you lose your premium—the price you paid for the contract(s)—if you don't exercise the option, which in our case is selling before the contract sunsets at the end of its corresponding expiration date.

We only trade Weeklys with either Same Day Expiration (SDE) or Next-Day Expiration (NDE). SDE is offered Monday, Wednesday and Friday, and as the name implies, go poof at the end of the corresponding session. Next-Day (NDE) options are available on Tuesdays and Thursdays, and continue for two trading sessions until the end of the next trading day, typically the following Wednesday or Friday assuming no holidays.

We don't hold our option contracts past the session we're trading regardless, we close our positions before the end of each day no matter what.

Why?

SDEs expire at 4:00 EST that session, but if you hold onto next-day options, you're subject to the following mornings pricing at open, whatever the post and pre-market forces deem it to be if you hang through the night. You won't want to lose sleep worrying whether your account might blow up by sunrise based on after-hours trading from overseas.

Option Pricing:

Bid Size	Price	Ask Size
	1.83	
	1.81	
	1.79	
	1.77	
	1.75	
	1.73	
	1.71	
	1.69	
	1.67	
	1.65	32
	1.63	55
	1.61	
	1.59	302
	1.57	138
	1.555	
	1.55	
1	**1.53**	69
127	1.51	
	1.49	
287	1.47	
	1.45	
	1.43	
	1.41	
89	1.39	
	1.37	
	1.35	
	1.33	
	1.31	
	1.29	

You pay an option premium, just like purchasing an insurance policy. The price you pay PER option contract is called the **strike price** and is shown, for example, as 1.53, which in real money means $153 per option contract. So if you bought or sold two contracts at that strike price, you would spend or make $306.

Where beginners often get confused, most products have a single, base price; but not options, each contract version has a price. Whether buying a call or put, options have multiple strike prices moving continually throughout trading based on the market action of buyers and sellers (supply and demand) for that particular contract, which are each numbered.

OTM, ATM, ITM, Oh My.

Option strike prices are characterized by the acronyms: **OTM, ATM** and **ITM**, which respectively stand for, **Out of the Money, AT the Money** and **In The Money**.

We trade mostly ATM—the only strike price that is at the money at any given time—but the price action movements affect whether each option rises or falls within that range. For example, in a sell-off, an originally ATM or ITM option could drop to OTM, and vice versa. OTMs become nearly worthless if they fall far enough regardless of market action, and ITMs become more valuable as the market supply for that option contract becomes more in demand (i.e. dwindling supply pushes up the price).

Furthermore the time value of all options "decays", in option lingo, over the course of the trading session. In other words, options steadily lose value as each nears expiration.

Time decay is known by its corresponding Greek, Theta. I don't want to dive into the Greeks here but just remember Theta = Time Decay, and despite profitability, options lose value no matter what as they approach expiration, which makes sense considering they expire worthless if you don't sell. In other words, the profit value shrinks as time progresses.

The practical implication, option strike prices decrease as they approach expiration even as individual calls and puts are profitable depending on their status related to being OTM, ATM or ITM.

Say a particular SPY call option contract is 2.50 ($250) at 10 a.m. based on SPY individual stock shares trading at $375. A few hours later, that same call option may now be priced at 2.10 ($210), even though SPY is still trading roughly around the same $375. As any session progresses, time decay (Theta) increases and options become cheaper compared to earlier in the session as they near expiration; however, the flip side, we don't stay in trades more than between one to twenty minutes because Theta chews into your profit spread every minute until expiration, so there's diminishing return as the session winds down.

We are purely day traders regardless of the option expiration date, not swing traders, who hold their positions for days, weeks and months.

ZRCE = Zone, Reversal, Confirmation, Entry

At the risk of fogging out your brain, I'll end with the most important acronym and analysis memory aid, that you will repeat to yourself while assessing the candle action on your charts. Don't worry, we'll cover this in some form the rest of this book, so just memorize the acronym so I don't have to write out every word over the remaining pages.

Zone, Reversal, Confirmation, Entry (ZRCE) represents our four-step confirmation, decision-making trigger for mentally accepting a trade before you physically click the buy button risking your money. ZRCE will become second nature.

I'm ending this chapter with a basic explanation and then covering in greater detail most of the rest of this book how ZRCE plays out in price action relative to the zones you identify and draw.

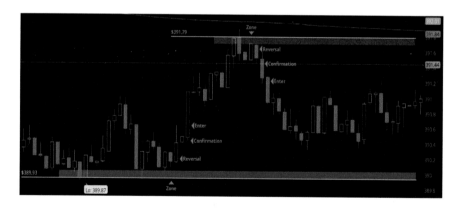

Each letter of ZRCE represents a candle acting upon and reacting to our ten-cent, supply and demand zones. The Zone and Reversal candles are opposite colors, depending on the price action (i.e. green and red or vice versa). The Zone candle touches or enters the zone you drew, the Reversal candle opposes, or rejects that first candle (opposite color). The Confirmation candle is the same color as the Reversal candle, as is your Entry candle. So the three final candles, RCE, are the same color (green or red depending on the direction) and reject the Zone candle.

A final key component of the ZRCE set-up, <u>the entire Confirmartion candle body,</u> but not any wicks, should ideally close OUTSIDE the zone before your Entry candle begins to form. I'll explain this next within the context of candle bodies and patterns but these are the basic ZRCE rules of the road.

Why does ZRCE matter?

Our four-step entry process prevents you from guessing, trading on a whim, and enables the chart time to tell you its story. Think of ZRCE as your security blanket for capital preservation, part of your risk management. Trading only major zones, relying on what the chart is telling us, entering only after recognizing ZRCE confirmation and multiple retests is how we make trading boring, yet extremely profitable by riding the coattails of the market makers.

We allow the chart to lead us by what you'll learn next.

6

Price Action and Zones

Price action not only forms each individual and group of candles but also the zones comprising areas of support and resistance. Price action births our chart.

Although not guaranteed, the candle's characteristics—body length, wicks, direction, color, speed forming, pattern grouping—give clues about what could potentially occur.

Even the candle wicks tell a story; think of long wicks as fishing poles, when the hedge funds reel in YOUR MONEY gobbling up stop losses to gain liquidity!

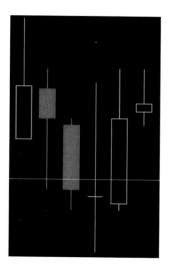

Wicks on either side of a small candle body represent a tug-of-war between bulls and bears. A candle without a body that resembles a cross or T, called a Doji, often portends a reversal, but not always.

Numerous books explain the history, naming and reading of these Japanese candlesticks, hence the Japanese labels for many of the candle types. While fascinating and indeed informative, breathe a sigh of relief our system doesn't require you to become a candlestick expert, which certainly won't hurt to learn if you'd like to research while you're awaiting your price alerts to trigger, but it isn't necessary.

Understanding a few candle basics relative to overall price action informs you enough to trade competently and confidently. The color of the candles (green buyers, red sellers), the up/down direction and the length of the candle bodies signal, when combined and reacting to the zones, what MIGHT happen as you analyze the volume forest from the individual candle trees (i.e. the overall trend/chart patterns versus the 5-minute/1-minute price action).

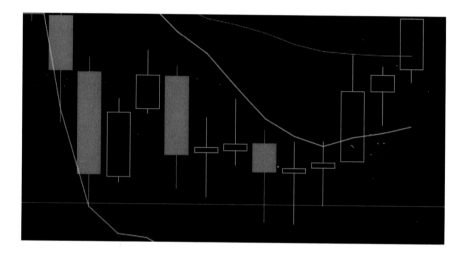

For example, a long candle body typically connotes higher volume and more rapid price movement (volatility); a shorter candle body, especially with wicks, generally demonstrates lower volume and less price conviction. A Doji is when sellers (bulls) and buyers (bears) fight price to a draw, so be on guard for what happens next, which could be a reversal and is at least a warning sign to be alert.

How the candles react individually and together to lines of resistance/support and the major/minor zones consequently formed is price action. We assess price action and apply our rules to decide when to enter and exit trades based on the price action story the chart tells us.

Before we pull the trigger, we decide our stop loss and take profit areas, review volume and the overall trend and finally apply our four-candle confirmation, ZRCE. <u>Your 100 percent trust in the process and discipline following your personal, risk management rules leads you into the Top 10 Percent of Traders</u>. Like golf, you will battle yourself to get there.

So those are the raw basics, now let's dive deeper into how any trade proves to you it's worth taking and the <u>multiple confirmations</u> (not just one) you will apply to master your analytical edge over speculative gambling.

The Waiting Game

Remember our trade execution goal, make your entries and exits so methodical you become bored. To trade like a sniper, you will wait, and wait longer, which is proof you're patiently picky and not impulsive.

How much waiting?

I've sat tight an entire day for the ideal setup. I've also gone days without trading. Sometimes when I spot a potential play on my chart but it appears choppy, I think, "Nope, I'm walking away until later because you don't deserve my attention", as if speaking to a petulant child.

And I urge you to physically get up and leave your computer, or work on something unrelated or watch a movie, because the Siren's Song of day traders, you will stare at the screen long enough to see something you like!

We seek quality over quantity while keeping everything simple (KISS = Keep it Super Simple). We reduce our probability of losing by entering fewer, but better profit plays which meet our strict, multiple confirmation rules. We don't stalk the screen all day and instead we pre-plan our trades and rely on our trading platform's price alarms. The biggest challenge will be managing yourself, which I cover in Chapter Nine and our coaches emphasize continually.

Magnetic Zones

Imagine the major zones as the Death Star in Star Wars, price action is continually pulled toward the major zones, and toward and through minor zones along the way. Remember the MDZ is the lowest priced zone, plus the 10-cent buffer, where the candles agree the price won't go any lower, and the MSZ is the highest priced zone, minus 10-cents, where buyers and sellers concur price won't go higher for the time being. The market makers agree those are the highest and lowest prices at that point.

What causes a break in this friction? The market makers boost their liquidity during accumulation phases by flooding the market with their huge positions in one direction or the other, either a rejection of the major zones, or a continuation through and development of new highs and lows.

What's known as consolidation (sideways chop) happens in the interim between major zone moves. Think of consolidation periods as a pressure cooker, we await price action that releases the pressure valve sending the option in one direction or the other.

The market makers have so much money they cannot shove all their chips in at once or the market price would swing wildly so fast nobody would trade, thus the zones take time to develop as a consequence of the insider's measured approach. In other words, lines and zones of support and resistance don't happen by sheer coincidence, and multiple times will be revisited and retested as the market makers generate capital.

The insiders can see stop losses and algorithms inform them when and how they can generate profit by milking retail traders and each other. We're essentially trading against programmed robots. Therefore we rely on confirming multiple times and using mental stops, critical for riding the hedger's coattails in the shadows without being scooped up in their liquidity net like those who place automated stops. (I cover this later.)

The large green and red candles are the market makers buying and selling respectively to push the price in their desired direction. While we cannot see stop loss orders, the market makers cannot hide from their huge volume moves; they can't do anything small, so that's our signal and we learn to recognize the price action and apply our confirmations to know when to enter and exit.

The most current major zones help predict where SPY is headed and the minor and replaced major zones are take-profit areas along the path to the opposing major zone or to a newly formed major zone. Imagine the minor zones as the net on a tennis court with the major zones as the baselines. <u>We use the candle formations on the 5-minute and 1-minute charts to inform where we're headed, and the 1-minute specifically for entries and exits based on our four-step confirmation, ZRCE</u>.

Now that you follow the theoretical, let's delve into how to analyze price action, recognize your entry criteria, and give your trade wiggle room to perform before reaching your take profit target or mental stop loss.

7

Analyzing Price Action
for Entries/Exits

Now let's put it all together and pull the trigger. <u>We use the five-minute chart for assessing the bigger picture, market trend (direction) and one-minute price action for confirming entries and exits.</u>

Remember this common sense (and likely intelligence insulting) albeit important mathematical fact: the five-minute candle is composed of five, one-minute candles (5 min = 5 x 1 min). Well duh, right?

Here's the point, you might lose sight in the heat of trading battle staring too much at the one-minute chart and miss the overall trend because of the lag in time of the five-minute candles forming FROM the one-minute candles, quite often each chart is briefly showing different color candles.

Sometimes you'll lose sight of this common sense difference focusing myopically on the one-minute chart, which could affect your planned entry and exit assessing trend if the five-minute is catching up on a reversal from or continuation through a zone. This would be like staring off the end of your hood without watching the road ahead. Patience pays, sometimes you must allow the five-minute candle to fully form to be sure of the trend, especially at pivot points as nothing goes up or down forever before reversing course.

We also monitor volume (more later) and ONE indicator of average volume, VWAP, pronounced "vee-whop". **VWAP is the Volume-Weighted Average Price**, the ratio plotted as a magenta line on our chart of the cumulative share price to the cumulative volume over a given time (i.e. the average price based on both price and volume at that time). You can add this fundamental study to your chart from your trading platform's chart settings.

IMPORTANT: VWAP is the ONLY indicator we use because it often reacts like a minor zone, but we don't trade off it alone as with major zones because its buffer is only one penny and VWAP is unpredictable. For that exact reason, we DO use VWAP as our closest take-profit line.

Trading off VWAP is the single most violated rule of the MK Supply and Demand System because sometimes it works out fine and others it bites you royally. All of my past students are nodding as you read this.

There are advanced plays incorporating VWAP as a redundant confirmation zone, but you will earn plenty without the risk by sticking to the core strategy. Just know VWAP is impactful enough to pay attention to, but don't fall prey to relying on it as a zone or you will regularly reduce your account balance.

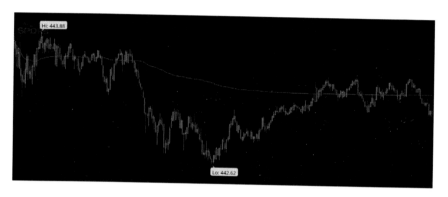

Furthermore, there are plenty of other indicators, like Fibonacci levels, MACD, RSI, but we don't use them. I'm not even going to explain them because I don't want you using them!

Why?

Because they lag, old news by the time they form whereas VWAP is a moving average. Technically, we could get away without even using VWAP, by simply relying on the candle pattern flow you plainly see, but VWAP provides a solid benchmark of the real time trend and serves as a take-profit area so it's helpful. I'll cover more about VWAP later when we dive into volume considerations but I just want you to be aware of and start to recognize that magenta line on your charts.

ZRCE in Action

Our supply and demand, four-step, ZRCE confirmation process replaces the need for fundamental analysis—following market news and events—which is stale by the time retail traders learn about and irrelevant to what smart money is doing regardless.

Our focus is purely what the candlesticks tell us in relation to the zones, volume and VWAP. We pre-plan our take-profit and stop loss areas, calmly execute, and then patiently watch as the chart tells us what to do next. The chart can only do three things: go up, down or sideways (consolidate).

Let's break down the following chart, which happens to include multiple examples of different trades within a short time. We'll zoom into each section of the same chart.

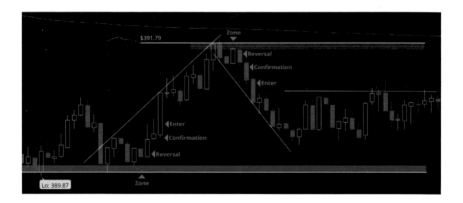

First thing when you open any chart, lean back and admire the forest, examine the macro view. Notice the candle colors, size and direction (e.g. how many of each, length, colors, direction). I've drawn basic trend lines, which you probably didn't need, to recognize the up, down and sideways price action.

When you look a little closer, you notice price action within the overall trends, same thing, up/down and sideways—the consolidated indecision we call "chop"—between the two major zones.

I'm going to zoom into and describe in detail each of the two trades I've diagrammed, neither is picture perfect but both are solid winners. You will learn quickly that trading is more art than science but the latter gives an edge over simply flinging paint onto the wall and hoping for a Sistine Chapel!

Four-Candle Entry: ZRCE on the One-Minute Chart

Before covering the trades above, let's review the core confirmation process of the Supply and Demand Strategy by identifying the ZRCE candles:

1. **Zone:** A green candle for calls and red for puts based on the prevailing trend. IDEALLY breaks, enters or taps the major zone; however, we still count IF/WHEN the candle gets within pennies of our 10-cent zones. Just be wary of fake-outs, which I will cover.

2. **Reversal:** The OPPOSITE color from the Zone candle. A large candle body conveys either strong sentiment or the insider's robot making a big move. Take a peek at the volume for clues.

3. **Confirmation:** The same color as the Zone candle. The body (not including wicks) ideally forms entirely outside the zone; however, trading being more art than science, we still count IF the Confirmation candle merely CLOSES (finishes forming) outside the zone (i.e. don't count if it closes within the zone). A Confirmation candle stacked atop the Reversal candle is a strong signal, but depending on size, could be taking you too close to your take-profit area to warrant the risk (more later).

4. **Entry:** Same color and should form atop the Confirmation candle. Give a few ticks but buy within the first eight to ten seconds or the train has likely left the station without you given strong sentiment demonstrated by volume as most trades last only minutes. Missing an entry due to a surging Entry candle often happens when the insiders flood the market with orders. Never chase because it often reverses just as quickly on the next candle; plus there's ALWAYS another trade.

So the final three candles are the same color, opposite of the first candle. HOW the candles are forming is arguably more important than WHEN for ensuring solid trades. Let's review our examples in more detail. Refer back to the four-steps as you look over the following graphics.

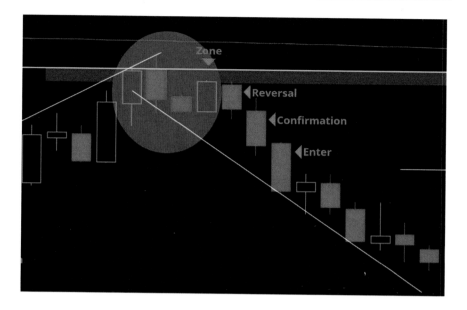

I'll start with the second trade, a put, that is a little cleaner and more "textbook", although it's still tricky because few plays are perfect, which is why I preach picky patience.

So what do you see?

First, we're trending upward (i.e. bulls/buyers/calls are beating bears/sellers/puts) heading toward our Major Supply Zone. Without the benefit of hindsight, we don't know in real time whether that uptrend will continue slicing through the zone creating a new MSZ higher, or whether bears/sellers will take over, reject the MSZ and begin to drive the price lower.

Our first clue, the opposing green and red candles exactly touch the blue MSZ price line, followed by the second red candle, indicating a possible reversal. In your mind, you'd be thinking, "Ah hah, major Zone green, Reversal red, Confirmation red, Entry red?.....nope.

Start over." In order to buy a put, you would've wanted to see the next candle be red and begin forming ideally beneath the previous candle. So we wait.

Here's where patience prevents you from jumping in too soon. Let the chart tell you when to enter. The following green candle is a do-over, our new Zone candle, during what we call a retest. Major zones are often retested multiple times, even a half dozen or more before going one way or the other, which is called a break-out from consolidation. Sometimes they aren't restested whatsoever, and the price shoots down or straight up again. Maintain discipline assessing price action, let the trade come to you.

In this scenario, the next green Zone candle is slightly lower than the previous green candle, a promising sign demonstrating a lower high. The wick on the previous Reversal candle also shows sellers wouldn't allow the price to go higher, another good sign, for a reversal and buying a put.

Then you get your clean, textbook ZRCE, put entry for a nice run down. You have pre-planned your take-profit and stop loss areas (Not yet shown, I'll cover this in detail shortly) and have your finger on the sell button for when price action tells you to exit the trade.

Notice the different colored candles and their wicks along the new downtrend. Each individual candle likely changed colors as it formed, but don't panic, because you've pre-planned your play like a sniper.

You're also keeping your eye on the five-minute chart (not shown) for the overall trend, remembering the one-minute candles are obviously forming faster so you must give the five-minute candles time to catch up, and your trade in general, wiggle room to perform.

Now let's look at the preceding trade on the same chart, which was trickier, and involved bending WITH our confirmation rules. We don't violate our rules, but sometimes we massage them so we don't miss profitable trades, based of course on your risk tolerance and experience.

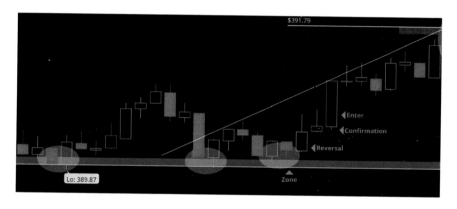

The first trade demonstrates how you must be both patient and alert. The candles challenged support at the green, major demand zone three times before bouncing higher, including a big momentum Entry candle that would have left you behind if you weren't ready to buy within the first ten seconds.

Look closely at the final retest. In real time, you'd have to judge whether to sit tight for another possible retest or a move lower, or jump in with a less than perfect ZRCE setup. Again, your volume indicator would've likely motivated you to enter but I will cover volume in more detail in the next chapter.

But on the final retest, the green Zone candle touched the MDZ but the next red candle negated it, so that red candle becomes the potentially new Zone candle contingent on what happens next. In this case, indeed, you have a green Reversal candle next and your Confirmation candle begins to form above its closing price so you would prepare to enter.

Some of you are likely thinking, "Hey, that red Zone candle didn't actually touch the zone!", and you're right! But here's when the art of trading trumps the science and we think to ourselves, "Close enough, I'm counting it", especially if you notice rising volume, a sign of strength. Remember, our zones are a ten cent average, the wick of that red candle came within three pennies so good enough. We wouldn't count it if it were another ten cents away; you've got a judgment call with anything around five cents.

What about the preceding zone taps, why not enter there?

The first two candles were solidly testing the zone but the red Confirmation, while briefly green, has a long wick and didn't clear the Reversal candle. The next small green candle demonstrates a lack of conviction, and while the price briefly moved higher, more times than not would be a fake-out. Same with the next retest before the final bounce, you can see how the buyers are trying to pull the market higher but just not quite ready and losing steam before the final retest, which was tipped off by increasing volume.

If you literally followed the ZRCE rules, you wouldn't have counted the final Zone candle and missed a profitable play. Know what? That would've been just fine because there's ALWAYS another trade so don't enter if YOU are not comfortable for any reason!

So totally up to you based on your risk tolerance but this is an example of when you might want to bend the rules. Plus you could've protected yourself with a tighter stop loss, which brings me to the next topics, deciding stops and take-profit (TP) areas. I'm going to briefly cover now and then explain nuances when discussing volume.

STOP my LOSS! (Risk Mitigation)

First, you will decide whether to set an automated stop (i.e. let your trading platform execute by entering a stop loss order); or what I suggest, use a "mental" stop by drawing a not-to-breach line or area on your chart, then selling manually if/when price action takes you there.

Either way you must be disciplined and stick to your stops! You can cancel an automated stop loss order just as easily as ignoring the line you drew on your chart and holding on too long to a loser. (And you will, most everyone learns this the hard way.)

And there are times when you might prefer one over the other depending on volatility and your take-profit tiers in order to protect your winnings so to speak (i.e. banking something over nothing in a fast moving market). Learn to use both of these methods and apply based on the situation.

You will ultimately decide based on your risk tolerance and the price action at that time; however, generally, I do NOT use automated stops because professional money sees them and always seems such a coincidence, when you enter a literal stop loss order, viola!, that's where you get filled every time, almost as if the insiders knew you were there and have an algorithm to snag you (because they do!).

Where do I set my line-in-the-sand, mental stop?

Again, depends on the market action and your fortitude sitting tight through sideways and backwards moves; <u>few trades go straight up or down</u> without pausing to consolidate or head fake. Why? Because the market makers are continually filling their coffers and setting up liquidity moves.

So while price action and your mental state during your trade will dictate, typically we establish our stops in one of three areas: bottom of Confirmation candle, leading edge of major zone, or the price line establishing the same major zone (i.e. top of zone for red MSZ, bottom for green MDZ).

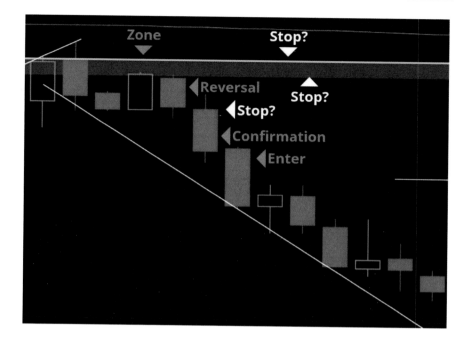

The trade, price action and your plan dictate where you stop out, which could change throughout a session. For example, your level of capital conservation will be much different at 100 contracts versus one contract, or certain times of the day like Power Hour. Or maybe you tire of sideways chop after ten minutes and wish to break-even or minimize your loss. And your mental stop can also move UP on the price ladder (known as a trailing stop) like a backstop, entirely away from the ZRCE candles, to protect surging profits and prevent you from getting too greedy before a big reversal snatches back any or all of your gain.

Among these three stop area options, getting out at your Confirmation candle would be most conservative, followed by the leading edge of the zone. If price action isn't moving quickly, give your trade more time to perform by letting it potentially back up to the price line of the zone. Volatility will dictate, one large candle in one direction or the other will affect your decision whether to stop loss or take profit. Think of both like riding a bucking bronco or surfing a wave, there will be a point when you've had enough and want to get out.

Remember too, not shown in these graphics, you will <u>keep your eye on the five minute chart as your guidepost</u>. We use the one-minute for deciding entries and exits, but the five-minute lights our path. If the five-minute is still favoring your trade, you might choose to hang longer (without getting too greedy) depending on your overall risk management plan. Generally you'll stick to your take-profit areas just as you do your stop loss lines.

<u>A common rookie mistake is holding onto losers too long (i.e. not honoring your stop) and bailing on winners too soon</u>. You must be disciplined and patient to give your trade time to mature. Granted, profit is profit and there's always another trade, but you don't want the individual amounts of your losers regularly exceeding the amounts of your winning trades because, even with a high winning percentage, your capital risk isn't worth your reward.

This is a good segue about when to cash your chips. While you want to give your trade wiggle room, you don't want to cling too long and risk a fast reversal.

Take My Profit

As with deciding your mental stop, your take-profit (TP) lines are pre-planned before you buy. You don't jump into a trade after spotting only ZRCE without also knowing in both directions where you might be going.

Just as with establishing your stops, you find areas on the one-minute chart where price action can meet resistance and possibly reverse, you also decide an ultimate take-profit line that, if everything goes swimmingly, you will call it a day and be ecstatic, regardless of whether the trade keeps improving!

Rarely do calls or puts ping pong straight from one major zone to the other, so your likely exit is a minor zone along the way, VWAP, or another former zone if a continuation and creation of a newer high or low. The five-minute chart and volume will inform and I'll cover that next, but for now here are basic take-profit levels.

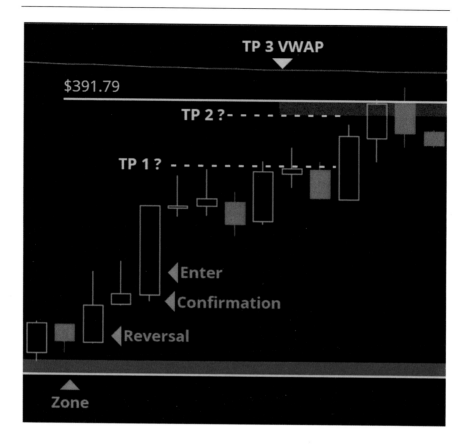

Let's pre-plan the first trade on the same chart we've reviewed. I didn't mark but your stops would be either the bottom of the Confirmation candle if you're being ultra conservative, or the top/bottom of the green MDZ, then you'd decide when to bail based on price action, volume and what the five-minute chart shows directionally.

Your take-profit lines are the nearest minor zones, a new major zone and VWAP.

I must confess, I'm cheating in this example because you obviously wouldn't be able to see the future candles (but wouldn't that be nice!).

For space considerations I'm drawing minor resistance levels from across the chart, off screen, much earlier in the session so I can make a point graphically without zooming out the chart too small to see. In other words, TP 1 and TP 2 were minor zones preceding this price action and the lines would've originated from the left out of view, which is a good time to mention, "Always look left" (on your chart screen) to discover previous lines of resistance and support for planning TP and stops.

You might also be thinking, why not use the previous red candle immediately before TP 1? There would in fact be small profit but you'd be committing the rookie mistake of panicking and getting out too soon without giving the trade time to run because your stop is not remotely threatened.

Bottom line, <u>you're the boss when to bail</u> but your pre-planning and watching the five-minute chart and volume should give you conviction to let this trade develop to your TP lines as you monitor the one-minute chart. Sometimes price action is moving so fast in your favor the candles surge right through your TPs, a "good problem" to experience; however, keep your finger on the sell trigger while letting the horses gallop a bit to see what happens.

Your TP 2 starts at the leading edge of the red MSZ but could be anywhere within the zone to the zone's top, price line depending on how fast the one-minute candles are forming, but give it a full sixty seconds to form and maybe the next one to start, then decide whether to sell.

Notice TP 3 doesn't have a question mark. In this example, VWAP is TP 3 and experience shows that would be the ultimate stopping point because it's so close to a major zone, and in fact, this trade reversed perfectly at the price line. The absolute most you could've made would've been if you just happened to sell at the tippy top of the red candle wick (doubtful). In all likelihood you probably would've sold when the green candle entered the zone and been quite thrilled with this trade.

But what if the candle had blasted through the zone up to VWAP, then what?

VWAP is always a danger zone, a wildcard. Even if a candle cut through VWAP, you'd likely want to sell immediately and not flirt with coin flip odds of a fast, large volume rejection downward. Continuing to hold beyond VWAP, especially in this example, would be unnecessarily risky, plus you attained your profit goal. <u>Always respect your plan in both directions</u>.

Patience Pays

I end this chapter by pulling you up for air from the minutiae to reinforce a few trade management principles.

<u>Patience pays in two ways, each by making you picky</u>. Patience either improves your profitability by taking fewer but better trades, yet also by preserving your capital when you don't feel right about a trade for whatever reason, including your mental state (e.g. bad mood,

fatigued, distracted, unconfident). Never beat yourself up sitting on the sidelines, there's ALWAYS another trade.

By the same token, don't let perfect be the enemy of good. Wait for the ZRCE candles to form but look at them as a whole entity within the overall chart trends, and don't get too myopic staring at the individual trees and miss the forest. In other words, maybe one of your ZRCE was the wrong color or too short/wicky, and cancels itself out, but maybe the next candle puts you back on track to complete the "four"-candle confirmation for a solid trade that just might not be picture perfect with consecutive candles.

Regardless, <u>patient pickiness prevents you from jumping in too early and getting caught by the insiders in a false move, while also enabling you to recognize when to still enter even if the ZRCE candles aren't perfectly in order but still justified by volume and the trend</u>. Experience will teach as your eyes read the story of the candle patterns. I will cover volume next.

At the end of each session, your charts should show only a pair of major zones because you've cleaned up as the day progresses. Your charts should be as clear as your mind.

8

Volume is Our Big Brother

The way Smart Money manipulates the market, you probably feel you're being watched by Big Brother, who knows your every move before you do. Volume helps level the field a little; volume is OUR big bro, BFF and wingman because professional money cannot hide from their large moves. We know it's them! Volume is our lifeguard or guardrail, a critical component finalizing our entries and exits.

How can you tell?

Let's examine a few general examples before drilling down. Forget technical analysis for a moment, your kindergarten eye will see it if you simply remember shapes.

By now you recognize candlesticks, the bar chart below shows volume with each bar representing its corresponding candle directly in line above it. What do you notice? Everything got ginormous in no more than sixty seconds (i.e. those are one-minute candles), and likely in the first few seconds of the candle forming. THAT my dear friendly traders, are the market makers either making your day or blowing up your play depending on whether you bought a call (green candle) or put (red candle); and you would've wanted to get out quickly in either event.

This basic example shows the insiders instantaneously boosting the price before taking it all back milking those stop losses. Actually, they're doing that in either direction to some unlucky retail traders because heads they win and tails you lose when they can see everyone's automated stop loss orders.

Again, you didn't need any particular specialized knowledge to recognize on the chart something went bigly up, then down immediately. What you will learn with experience is how volume combined with the shape, speed and direction of the candles individually and within groupings (patterns) tells a story. And while sometimes the candle shapes and patterns can fool us—like when a Doji candle is NOT a reversal—BIG MONEY can never hide from tipping its hand during BIG VOLUME. We've at least got that going for us.

Let's go deeper so you can learn how to read volume as a decision-supporting aspect of assessing price action. Remember this basic tenet as you proceed: <u>volume always demonstrates conviction</u> (i.e. whether candles support or lack). That's why it's such an important confirmation and rejection signal.

Volume is the ONLY leading indicator

Noodle that. Anything else carries some element of time delay, even our near and dear, VWAP is an AVERAGE. But volume is happening right this second, which is what makes it so powerful in combination with candle formations.

And what volume deciphers is the validity of price action, whether true or false. Price action by itself merely reveals buying and selling, but not necessarily legitimacy of the move. Support and resistance lines are the cornerstone of technical analysis, and combined with volume, you'll know the strength of a candle or pattern of candles, or whether a fake out.

Entire books have been written about analyzing volume in combination with chart patterns; however, rest assured we're clinging to our KISS (Keep it Super Simple) Principle. Think of volume as a backstop, a final reality check of your ZRCE confirmation.

Simply, <u>volume tells us whether what we're seeing in the one-minute and five-minute price action is legit or possibly a head fake of what's to come next.</u> Again, the insiders cannot hide from volume, which tips their hand every time whether a break-out or rejection is imminent from a period of consolidation.

Where to next?

In the spirit of not overcomplicating, <u>this is all we're trying to figure out about price levels from our "volume analysis", a simple double check of the candle action and trend direction</u>. Rising volume bars with increasing candles stacking upon one another is a no brainer, but most often you'll spot irregularities, for example a really tall candle with below average volume, and with experience will be able to tell whether a genuine or invalid price move (i.e. sit out or stay in).

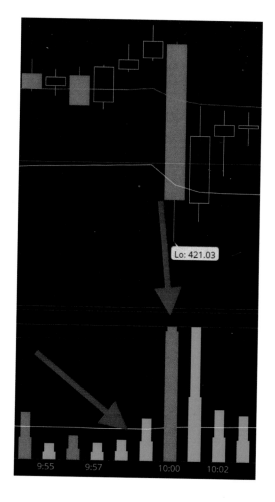

In this example, the yellow line on the volume bar chart represents the moving average volume. Notice what happens at EXACTLY 10 a.m. in relation to the one-minute chart and the corresponding bar chart.

Retail traders boosted price higher, above the magenta VWAP line, then at 10 a.m. sharp an automated algorithm pumped the market with puts, slurped stop losses and drove the price to a session low before an immediate about-face in the opposite direction to gain even more hedge fund liquidity. Then the volume dust settled with price below VWAP for the time being. That all happened in two minutes and the main surge likely happened in less than ten seconds, sometimes in three ticks.

There's not much you can do when moves are that sharp and faster than you can click your mouse; however, you will be able to support a buy or sell decision based on noticing increasing or decreasing volume bars as the chart story unfolds. Price action must be supported by its corresponding volume, cause and effect. In other words, volume reveals activity and validates price within a market insiders are continuously manipulating.

Volume gives us our bearings whether the candle shapes are justified. In the example above, that huge move was manufactured by the market makers and wasn't reflective of pure supply and demand, buying and selling. If you were in that trade, you experienced either good or bad luck depending on what you bought, and you'd want to sell pronto regardless.

Here's a basic, cause and effect example of a good, volume-supported trade; I've purposely kept the chart clean without drawing zones, so you can focus simply on the candles and volume bars.

Notice how green buyers drove up the price, above the magenta VWAP line, just barely avoiding a Doji candle draw with red sellers—the wicks on either side of the short candle body demonstrate buyers/bulls were losing steam, and the below average, up-down volume bars confirm.

Then the red sellers/bulls entered, increasing red volume drove price down as the volume bars stair-stepped up in the first half hour of trading (10 a.m. EST). The increasing volume of the put trade as the candles cascaded downward supported this quick trade and strong move.

The green candle at the bottom, still with decent volume, is a possible anomaly (i.e. insiders testing for buyers) as price struggled back to VWAP, then volume bled off and price consolidated in a period of sideways chop.

Volume reveals strength of price movement, whether the supply and demand reactions are genuine or when the market makers are mopping up for liquidity. Without insider manipulation, the market doesn't naturally stop dead in its tracks and immediately reverse course, whenever that happens it's a glaring red flag. Be cautious acting immediately (outside of Power Hour and other special circumstances like Fed days) without checking volume.

At the same time, don't obsess over volume, we're only trying to figure out one thing, are the candles valid or is this a trick? Here are some examples when you would be on guard.

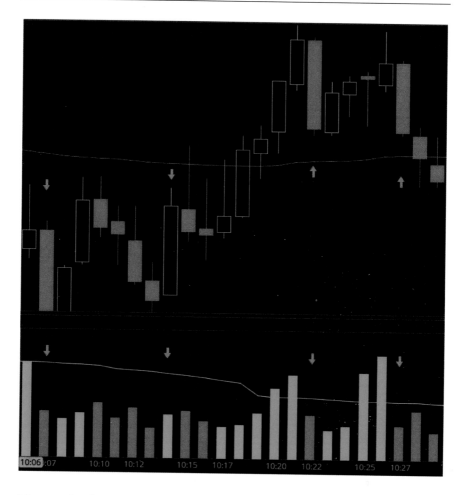

Notice the long candle bodies with correspondingly below average volume (i.e. the yellow line on the volume bar chart is average volume). Those types of moves are dubious. Conversely, starting at 10:17 a.m. is what you hope to see, increasing volume with strong candle formations, mindful that VWAP is always a caution zone.

See the friction between buyers and sellers during this half hour? Compare the colors, volume bars and candle shapes/patterns. A grade-schooler can do this so don't overcomplicate, but from a macro view, the buyer bulls were winning at this time, a clear upward trend of higher prices. Double-checking volume at each stage (because hindsight is 20/20) substantiates the price action.

Here's an example of a tough, choppy day, when the hedgers popped in here and there to slurp up automated stop losses.

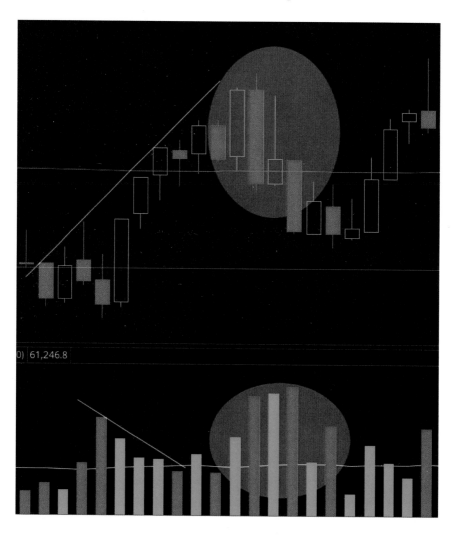

Notice this bullish uptrend with falling volume. The buyers were winning, tugging price higher, but volume declined as the uptrend lost steam around VWAP. Then the hedgers arrived, leading many traders to think the price was moving higher but wham!, down it went in seconds, then back up the next minute as pro money's automated algorithm vacuumed in each direction. This is a prime example of why VWAP is often a take profit point because it often reacts as a one-cent, major zone.

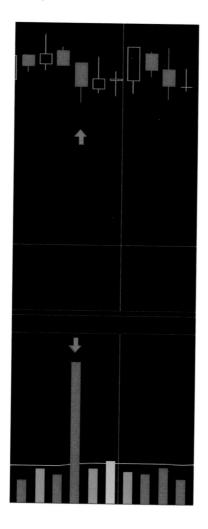

Finally, here's a huge, out-of-the-blue, volume move with a smallish-to-typical sized candle. Big Money was likely testing whether retail traders would join in before reversing course and collecting stop orders. Each of the previous examples are anomalies, a red flag warning either to sit out or get out.

<u>Seek to answer whether volume is confirming the price action you see.</u> You ideally want any trend up or down (i.e. green candles stacking upward, or red candles cascading downward) accompanied by rising volume proving conviction of the move (i.e. cause and effect, effort and result). In other words, you want to see the length of the candle somewhat match its corresponding volume bar (long/tall, small/short). Even without the yellow line showing average volume, you can eyeball the volume bar's height and assess whether volume is below, around or above its rolling average.

Bottom line: Is volume buying or selling, and should I join or get out? Is the volume effort validating the price action result? And don't forget to double check volume on both charts, are the one-minute and five-minute saying the same thing?

I'm stopping here because, as mentioned, whole books have been written about volume analysis, which endangers maintaining our KISS approach. However, a few final thoughts as you get to know and rely upon volume as your wingman.

<u>The markets spend far more time moving sideways within a range, consolidating, than going up or down. Volume helps you recognize when a break could be imminent.</u>

As you gain experience, you learn about many types of candlesticks and patterns (e.g. Bullish Engulfing, Hammers, Hanging Man, Pennant, Shooting Star, Triangles, etc.); and while "nice to know", you don't truly need beyond your kindergarten eye for shapes.

Remember, <u>start with the candles and zones first, THEN notice whether volume is validating market sentiment</u>. Volume divulges whether it's us or THEM, the automated algorithm manipulators. Monitoring volume can save your day, and trading account! As Mamma always said, "It's better than noth'n!"

FEAR and GREED underpin every bit of supply and demand, price action between professional money and retail traders. No matter what the chart reports, those two emotions are ever present as bulls battle bears.

As we round for home, I conclude with THE most important chapter.......

9

Rule Your Mind

Welcome to the single hardest aspect of trading, managing yourself. Seriously. A majority of trading gurus insist success is adhering to the proper strategy and tactics, but nope, it's all between the ears no matter which system you follow. You can screw up even by following proper procedure if your mind isn't right.

"What, all on me? Are you kidding?" You're here chiefly for one of two reasons, you're a raw beginner or you've experienced less than stellar results using another strateg(ies).

Those in the latter camp likely already acknowledge and accept that 90 percent of trading is psychological, a battle against yourself. Once you learn the technical how, what and when, then it all becomes WHO, which be YOU!

Why? Because trading, whether and when to buy and sell, distills to YOUR decision-making, and that's impacted by your personal history, emotional makeup and human traits baked into everyone's biological brains.

In regard to the latter, professional money figured this out decades ago, and began pouring millions into behavioral and physical brain research that morphed into new fields in research psychology, primarily what became known as Behavioral Science and its sub-genres of Behavioral Economics and Behavioral Finance.

While the roots of "behavior science" began as far back as the 1900s, the psychological aspects of how people deal with money and rewards started in the Sixties and Seventies and then really took off after the 2008 financial crisis. Research scientists won Nobel Prizes studying cognitive biases—mental shortcuts called heuristics (e.g. Endowment Effect, Hindsight Bias, Loss Aversion, Optimism Bias,

Sunk Cost Fallacy)—and nobody is immune because it's hardwired into our caveman brains.

Now why do you think Big Money would want to know why and how little old me and their competitors make the decisions we do time after time about money and taking risks? Hmmmmm.

That's enough of the theoretical, let's uncover what you already have or will experience with this far-from-exhaustive list:

- Losses: you will lose, everyone does
- Fear: Many variations including FOMO (Fear of Missing Out), competitiveness, comparing yourself to others and chasing trades.
- Overconfidence/Overoptimism: from believing you cannot lose to seeing patterns where none exist.
- Perfectionism: Thinking too much, paralysis by over-analysis, allowing perfection to be the enemy of good, mostly due to some type of fear of losing or lack of conviction.
- Self-loathing: Defeatism. You never do anything right, beating yourself up. There's always another trade but you can't let go of the one you didn't win.

We ALL experience some form of these. Trading can and will be extremely stressful if you fail to manage your mood as an emotional balance beam. Remember our mission, keep it KISS and BORING, but the mental and emotional hiccups happen periodically. Nobody totally avoids, not even me. I have my own unique challenges, we all do and step one is accepting that reality.

Trades Don't Care Because......

Trades are just things, which go up, down and sideways. Obviously, right? The trade doesn't care about your house payment, personal issues, background, hopes or dreams. It's just a trade, which are? Quite literally calls and puts, but what do those products we're buying and selling comprise? Supply and demand within a market of who? Buyers and sellers, but who are they?

People, individuals with their own stories, problems, talents and experiences buying and selling. And what are each of us doing simultaneously, whether for ourselves or a hedge fund? We are DECIDING. <u>At the most micro level, we are individually making choices to do or not do something in seconds.</u>

Mix it all together and that's the arena we're competing within, and chiefly AGAINST not others, but OURSELVES and how we perform regardless of what anyone else is doing, despite the reality that what others do impacts us and how we react to the candles.

Therefore, how we manage ourselves dictates our win rate, profitability, time freedom and ultimately.....drum roll....our contentment and sense of balance in life. Pretty damn heavy, huh?

Some of you might be thinking, "This is all nice to know but so what?" Understanding and accepting this is paramount.

The trading upshot, <u>you must get to the point mentally that you don't care about the trade</u>. Wait, come again. Indeed, to trade like a sniper, you need to become as emotionless as possible, even bored! Snipers are detached from what's on the other end of the barrel peering through their rifle scope.

Some successful traders actually think they'll lose heading into a play. How is that helpful!?! Because they've accepted intellectually and emotionally that they "could lose" and they don't care having accepted the risk after thoughtfully following their plan (i.e. they've done all they can do, now it's up to the Market to confirm their competitive edge). They're absolutely willing to risk and lose what they're spending without breaking a sweat, trembling or crying.

In a sense, they don't care because the trade is just a thing (i.e. "ain't nothin but a thing"), and it doesn't matter what the Market is doing, because they're prepared technically (knowledge, tactics), mentally (strategy, plan) and emotionally (calm, neutral mindset).

Emotional Messiness

Now you know the benchmark, be a robot just like the market maker's algorithms; but what's our human reality? Here are examples of what you will or already have experienced, and even veterans backslide.

Each of the following is rooted in some form of anxiety/fear or greed, and there's crossover.

- **Chasing:** The candle train left the station without you and you're determined to catch up, which is a sure fire way to meet head-on a reversal. Resist the urge because your profit margin was already sapped after you missed the boat the first ten seconds. Chasing is a form of FOMO, whether comparing yourself to others' success or perceived lost profit you "could've/should've made".

- **Gambling**: Could rise to addiction but the garden variety, risking money you shouldn't spend, including cash for current bills or your long term retirement/college savings. "Going for broke" rarely pans out. Impatience is another form, for example, jumping the gun entering on a Confirmation candle on a non-Doji play. Speculating on the direction of price action seeps in first before you begin breaking your trading rules becoming undisciplined to "make it happen!" and avoid "missing out". IF you are scared about losing the amount of money you're risking, you are gambling.

- **Late Entry/Early Exit**: Common for beginners and the fearful, marked by bigger losses relative to higher profit per trade (i.e. the opposite of what it should be), and rooted in trading anxiety. You lack conviction even in the face of clarity when entering the trade, freak out even though you're in profit and the candles are nowhere near your stop loss, and bail for small profit without giving the trade time to perform. We've ALL been here and sometimes this self-corrects with more practice and live trading experience; however, if it's an ongoing problem, your risk and reward is totally backwards and you're likely frustrated. There's absolutely nothing wrong with small profits, unless that's the rule rather than exception.

- **Over-Trading**: Could be fear, greed, frustration or any combination. In our system, you should be extremely picky and trade ONLY the major zones until you become experienced enough to earn a living day trading and have play money for more advanced trades. Until you are winning over 70 percent of your trades and consider day trading your full-time occupation, you shouldn't place more than three trades daily, with one or NONE the most common journal entry.

- **Revenge Trading**: "I refuse to lose!". You are ticked off, you just knew that candle was supposed to go the other way, it didn't and you're no quitter, not ending the session on a crappy loss. Or even more dangerous to your account, there's a certain amount you MUST make daily and you're in catch-up mode.

- **Sloppiness**: Fear and greed may only be in the background of this primary feeling of overwhelm. Fatigue, outside worries, distractions, feeling physically unwell, etc. overload your mind and cause you to mess up, even clicking the wrong button to buy the opposite of what you intended. We all brain cramp periodically but sit out when you're out of sorts (or practice). And also don't beat yourself up for missing a session, perceive instead as a profitable day of capital preservation, not risking a dime of your account balance!

The inner vibe you experience when these occur—and trust me it will and still does in times of weakness for everyone, even successful traders —is the trade actually feels forced and uneasy; you even physically feel the stress inside your gut, shaking, sweating, chest tightness, etc. My first few big money plays, when I was unemployed and quite literally rolling the dice with our remaining savings, my hand trembled so forcefully I could barely operate the mouse!

Seeing Things

Our brains evolved to seek patterns where none actually exist. Long ago we watched caveman Bob try to pet a saber tooth tiger to a rather messy end, so over centuries of neurobiological adaptation, our fight or flight responses developed to preserve our physical health.

Candlesticks and charts are patterns, so what gives?

Even if you don't make a single mistake and enter a picture perfect ZRCE trade, you can potentially and WILL lose every so often; however, following the Supply and Demand system over a SERIES of accurate entries improves your <u>statistical probability of success</u> (key phrase), <u>by focusing on FEWER trades off only major zones</u>.

Therefore being prepared, and even expecting to lose, by unemotionally adhering to our trading procedure and being disciplined with your own trading rules (e.g. not trading when tired or distracted) increases your odds of winning over seventy percent of the time because you won't trade as often so your chances of succeeding are better.

I've spent the majority of this book teaching you the what, when and how, now you must contemplate and figure out the most important part because.......the trade doesn't care.

Your BIG WHY?

I recounted within the first few pages why I began trading. I've coached hundreds of students and we typically discuss this within a couple of calls, and I rarely have to ask, their motivation spills out as if a pressure valve releases.

One student got laid off annually before the holidays but for a much different reason than my experience. Steven was a union bridge painter in the New York metro, and the work became too dangerous during the wetter, freezing months. He experienced coworker friends plunge hundreds of feet to their deaths. He began day trading during his down time between projects just to earn extra income, but then he had a baby boy and no longer wanted to risk his literal life at work.

Now that's a rather dramatic example of career transition! Some might argue he only had one choice as a father. Most everyone wants some form of time freedom and unlimited earning potential. That's a given for as long as multi-level marketing and side hustles have existed.

What you want to know is your CORE why besides money and time off. Regardless of how seemingly mundane (e.g. something to do to supplement retirement), you should understand your primary motivation, or why bother anxiously staring for hours at a computer?

I will guide you down that discovery path figuring out your highest, best purpose.

Why will it matter? The clarity of knowing and accepting your main reason for learning this skill fortifies your emotional trading clarity, which is THE key to your success or failure. Clear your mind and your fanny will follow as you develop a sniper's approach to pulling the trading trigger.

6 W(hy)s

The Six Whys (6 W's) is simple and effective introspection (i.e. soul searching) for figuring out your core reasoning for decisions or personal cause and effect. Similar to legal contract writing that strives to answer with each clause, "If not, then what?", the Six W's distills to your baseline WHY?

The method involves asking yourself, "Why?" no less than half a dozen times and contemplating the "real reasons" you are doing or not doing something. Sounds simple enough but you'll be surprised what you discover about yourself if you follow the procedure correctly and devote honest time and energy to this reflection, which borders on meditation.

The ground rules for this self-analysis:

1. You begin by formulating the core question you will ask yourself, as specifically as possible. For example, "Why is

[this] important to me?", "Why am I doing [this]?", or for our purposes, "Why do I want to day trade for a living?"

2. While this self discovery is labeled the Six W's, you can ask as many Whys as necessary and, if you find yourself stopping at half a dozen or less, you're probably not there yet, so take timeout and pick up later.

3. Feel free to also ask logical follow ups of Who, What and How as 6 W's is simply a naming convention.

4. <u>Do not slop through this</u>, don't start when tired, distracted, overwhelmed, etc. or you are wasting your time. Find a relaxed, thought-provoking setting, and this activity pairs well with wine.

5. <u>MUST DO: Physically write your answers on paper.</u> The act of writing results in a brain benefit better than typing or merely contemplating. We're going old school so invest in a spiral notebook or legal pad!

6. Do NOT limit yourself to completing in one attempt, although do not interrupt your momentum if your brain is flowing. Don't "slow the mo" if you're rolling.

7. <u>Do NOT edit your written answers, brain dump, let your mind lead you.</u> Jot down every thought no matter how tangential or seemingly trivial, and underline key thoughts because any word or phrase could unlock the kingdom.

8. WHEN you feel you've reached your limit, ask one final WHY? If coming up empty, you've likely found your answer.

9. REVIEW later. Put your notes aside and revisit another day after your mind has settled and slept on it. (Your brain processes overnight as you sleep, you might very well awaken overnight with more thoughts, so keep your notes near your bed.)

How will you know when you've arrived at your core answer?

First, you will feel mentally tapped out, maybe even emotionally whipped, like you just studied for an important test. Additionally though, you will also feel satisfied with your answer. You'll just know in other words, despite feeling foggy from all the mental heavy lifting.

Let's review a generic example of how this thought train might travel.

#1 WHY do I want to day trade for a living?

Not yet sure, seems crazy risky, don't know I could earn enough. I'm generally interested in the financial markets and keep up with economic news; but, I've always been a buy-and-hold investor. I admire Warren Buffet, certainly envy his bank account! However, I'm intrigued by day-trading, how anyone makes a living at it, and options in particular because I'm somewhat familiar with option contracts for other assets like real estate. I saw the Facebook ad, which reminded me of a trader friend who seems successful. I want to explore more because maybe this is a path for me too if I can understand it.

#2 But WHY?

Burned out at work. Can barely tolerate any aspect of my job, spending long hours for what feels like nothing. I actually feel empty at the end of every workweek. Meanwhile, my trading friend seems content, vacations multiple times a year, seems to lack for nothing. Hell, I'm lucky if I can take off one week, then I'm too tired to go anywhere.

#3 WHY not just get another job?

Lost that loving feeling for what I do. Not sure what else I can do that would pay the bills. Worn out by customers and office politics. Need a fresh start doing something I enjoy, with earning potential and relying ONLY on ME. I've always been a creative problem-solver but now I'm totally stuck, extremely frustrated I cannot think myself out of this.

#4 WHY not start a business?

NO time, no capital and nothing I really care about. I tried a few side hustles to earn extra, but didn't have enough discretionary hours to make it work without totally abandoning my family! Plus customers, ugh. Being "your own boss" is mostly a myth; you need customers so they're your boss. I would simply be trading one set of annoying people (boss, coworkers) for another.

#5 What appeals about trading?

From reading and watching a few videos, day trading seems to check all my boxes aside from the market being open during my work hours. (I'd need to figure that out, how to make worthwhile).

But the more I learn about how options work (leveraging more shares for less), trading grows on me (if I can tolerate the risk) because I enjoy learning new things, there's potentially unlimited income (and loss!) and time flexibility to do whatever I want. Plus it's a skill I can develop that nobody else can undermine!

#6 WHY or HOW important is that?

Self-mastery is important to me because I don't like relying on others, been disappointed multiple times and even burned a few, plus I've always enjoyed competing against and improving myself in sports, working out, and most every outside interest.

That's among the reasons I feel so trapped at work, I'm dying on the inside. I'm not having fun and my work is now simply a means to an end, a J-O-B. I can't even remember the last time I was excited about going to work. I'm doing the bare minimum and not proud of myself!

As long as I maintain interest in something, I strive to be my best and remain engaged. Once I lose interest, I lose focus and feel imprisoned. Boredom is my enemy. I need a new cause!

#7 How would trading satisfy?

From what I can tell, there's always something to learn, to make me a better trader for my own personal bottom line. Seems like it's a game against myself, sort of like golf, and my success is totally up to me and my effort without the interference of anyone else.

And if I can earn enough to pay my bills, I'll enjoy freedom of time like my friend, who doesn't just vacation, but coaches multiple sports and is actively involved in our community. I can work from wherever and trading hours are the only constraint.

Plus the money potential! Could certainly use more coin to get ahead and provide for my kids the advantages I enjoyed.

#8 What advantages, why important?

My parents and grandparents paid for my college so I didn't have to take on a nickel of debt, a tremendous gift I've always appreciated and never forgotten. The only "loan repayment" stipulation is that I pay-it-forward and do the same for my kids and grandchildren.

From the first day of my career I've done all the traditional things, dutifully contributed to my company 401k and opened college savings plans, but I don't feel I'm on pace to grow those accounts enough for both retirement and paying multiple tuitions, when the costs of the latter is increasing faster than my balances.

It's extremely important to keep my promise to my folks, doing my best but not sure I can, which saddens me. I will feel like such a failure if I can't do for my kids what was GIVEN to me, a carefree college education. All I had to do was attend class, study and maintain good grades, not much to ask for a free ride.

#9 How will trading help you accomplish?

Unlike passive investing, day trading is solely up to my performance regardless of whether the market goes up, down or sideways—I began exploring day trading after the S&P finished up the exact afternoon a war started! I just need to learn how to do it without gambling my savings. I don't want to touch my retirement and education funds.

Thankfully the barriers to opening a trading account are the lowest I can find compared to the startup funds necessary for anything beyond multi-level marketing (which requires customers!!!).

I don't plan to ever risk a cent of my retirement or college savings for trading; even so, my final take when I begin to cash out those accounts will be impacted the most by whatever the economy just happens to be going through at that time (recession, inflation, worse?), which doesn't make me feel warm and fuzzy. Whereas there's always money to be made (and lost) trading options every single day the market is open.

I'm actually getting excited about this! For the first time in years, I feel HOPE that maybe this is indeed my answer.

#10 Need another WHY?

I'm going to think on this overnight but no, I feel in my heart day-trading checks all the boxes and might be my solution. I'm going to take the next step!

Postmortem:

I purposefully picked that word for the header (autopsy) because the Six W's will indeed feel like a death and revival!

You will deconstruct your old life and chart your new course, even if ultimately it doesn't whatsoever involve trading. I encourage you to go through that exercise no matter what: now, in the future and also share with others you care about, like your kids, for their major life decisions. Teach another person and brain science shows you'll ingrain in yourself.

A couple final points, I wrote a very basic, generalized example trying to resonate with as many readers as possible. In practice, this introspection will be <u>extremely specific and personal to you</u> as you drill down and SHOULD include any number of personal, relational and health considerations. Expect to become emotional, which is how you'll know you're doing it right and getting somewhere.

Remember you complete this WRITTEN introspection without editing or proofing, let it go and flow! Take your time, there's no deadline. <u>YOU are the only audience so don't hold back as if writing for someone else</u>. Pretend you're being interviewed and talk it out to yourself. I wrote formally and grammatically for a book, but this isn't a literary project so just jot notes and sentence fragments since you know what you mean.

But put aside once tapped out and return again afresh for one last look. Trust me, you'll know when you're "done, done." You'll feel it.

Your Minutely Rate

Let's come up for air and describe how your core WHY practically relates to the definition of what we call work. You exchange your skill and time (output) for a wage (pay). That's work, and it's helpful to remember it simply that way for what I'm about to describe.

No matter how you're paid—hourly, salary, commissioned—your income can be broken down into a unit of what your time is worth annually, monthly, daily, hourly, etc. Every dollar and minute of your life carries an opportunity cost, an economic term, which are the alternatives you could choose instead with your time and money. For example, you can spend your dollar or save, invest, bury, donate, etc. Same with your time, every single thing you do comes at the expense of something else you COULD be doing, especially if money isn't a concern.

So how much are your minutes worth? Might seem absurd to consider unless you've dealt with health problems, or taken care of someone, when the minutes seem excruciating. How much are minutes worth to an Olympian or race car driver who wins or loses by a hundredth of a second?

Unless you believe in reincarnation, we're only on this orb once. The value of your minutes comes into fine focus once you compare laboring for The Man versus ME Inc.

Many life coaches epouse "find your passion", which I feel is bovine scattery and impractical. Maybe for some whose paid work is a cause (e.g. adult literacy, clean water, ending childhood hunger, combatting addictions), OK, I'm good with that; but, for the majority of us, we must find something we're engaged with and adept at that pays a livable wage with reasonable hours devoted to what we call work.

Do you currently enjoy that type of wealth, enjoying your minutes working at what you're doing for your wage?

The balance of your non-labor day is where I believe "passion" resides, and that's time with friends, family and making happy memories. As the saying goes, nobody ever engraved on their tombstone, "If only I could've worked more."

Money affords opportunity and the capacity to solve problems, like buying a home, traveling, or paying for car repairs and medical bills. Therefore true wealth is foremost, your personal and family's health, followed by freedom of minutes to do anything you choose. That's the leverage power of money, <u>free agency to dictate your opportunity cost determining YOUR minutes.</u>

We're big fans of leverage in our system, using less cash to buy more SPY shares via options, and keeping everything KISS for trading more contracts over fewer candles for a higher winning percentage. We follow our rules because we understand the more frequently we place trades, the higher probability of loss. Conversely, the fewer, disciplined trades we take, eventually with higher contract amounts, the more we earn in less time in a beautiful marriage between cash and time leverage, which ultimately develops your personal freedom. See it?

Your Mindset

So I've explained the theory, strategy and tactics behind our MK Supply and Demand system, which truly is just the start. Our coaches tailor lessons to your life circumstances as well as teaching more advanced tactics; but ultimately, after you master a sound foundation of basics through practice and figure out your core WHY for doing this, you alone will decide and develop the most critical component that will make or break your account within our overall system, your personal trading rules (i.e. your literal decision every single trade of whether to buy or sit out based upon your mindset at execution).

In other words, we don't simply jump right in just because we recognize an ideal ZRCE setup. Your mind must be right as well, or you'll make simple but possibly costly mistakes (e.g. losing track of whether you have on Auto Send, mistakenly drawing support and resistance lines on the wrong chart) because you're distracted or tired. Trust me, it happens.

I conclude this chapter with some trading truisms you can rely on to develop your own personal dos and don'ts. As with your ultimate WHY, <u>your personal rules are specific to your life</u>.

Maybe there's a certain time or day you shouldn't trade because you won't be your best for whatever reason, you must write that down and adhere to it without FOMO because, if not, you WILL lose money more often than not. For instance, some top performers do not trade the final hour, Power Hour, due to volatility and huge, split second moves by the market makers, others may never trade when kids are home, or if they don't get a certain amount of sleep.

Bottom line, <u>be your optimal best when trading</u> because it will affect your bottom line.

Trading Maxims

Develop your own rules incorporating these foundational truths:

- Anything can happen on any single trade or session.
- <u>There is ALWAYS another trade</u> (Don't flog yourself over losses or missed plays.)
- EVERYONE loses, risk always exists.
- The normal uncertainty of the stock market promises you will have negative days, but those are not bad days <u>IF you didn't violate your trading rules.</u>
- EVERY trade, outcome and moment is UNIQUE and has NO relationship to anything in the past (i.e. same probability as coin flips).

- Expectations kill accounts.
- <u>NO sure things. Our minds are wired to see patterns where none exist. Our correct predictions are merely happenstance.</u>
- Each informed prediction from my analysis is still always an educated guess.
- Our Supply and Demand Strategy is an edge, nothing more than <u>a higher probability of one thing happening over another from a random distribution</u> of wins and losses for a given set of variables, but no guarantee.
- Rid myself of DESIRE and let the market lead. I cannot CREATE a trading opportunity, the market must present one.
- What others are doing is irrelevant to my bank account.
- The NEXT session or trade is ALWAYS a NEW opportunity.

Monitor Your Mindset:

What you measure can be improved with recognition and corrective action. Journaling every single trade, even simulated, is critical for developing skill as with performance reviews for anything. **Journaling is truly more about managing your mindset** than the transaction nuts and bolts of your trades.

And doesn't have to be fancy but absolutely should be detailed, including tracking your energy level, emotional bearing and time of day for each trade. Use a spreadsheet, legal pad or any number of trade journaling apps, but do NOT let this slide because you will determine over a series of trades your strengths and weaknesses from which you'll ultimately develop, refine and periodically update with experience your personalized trading style and rules atop the MK Strategy.

What should your journal entries include? I won't completely specify because this is an instance where more is better and over time you'll figure out what's important to you, but obviously you'll track basics of entry/exit price and times, trade duration, profit/loss and generally anything describing what you did right or wrong. As a basis for starting, click MauriceKenny.com/vip-trading-journal to learn more and download our version.

As you practice and then execute real money trades, remember the whole point is maintaining DISCIPLINE, and journaling tracks that very thing if you <u>honestly assess yourself immediately after every single trade</u> whether simulated or live. Take time out after closing your position and notate in detail how you did while fresh in mind. Don't wait! Journaling right away also prevents you from chasing another trade and enables you to decompress.

We track wins and losses differently within the MK Strategy, not simply whether you profited or lost, but <u>did you follow YOUR rules</u>? When you trade incorrectly but it works out, that's simply good fortune, but should still feel like a loss because you violated your plan.

When you gamble or do things wrongly, you're relying on arbitrary possibility (happenstance, good luck) instead of probability (strategic edge). Bolster the latter by being disciplined. Choosing the right path may take longer, but the probability of success is greater, especially with fewer, higher quality trades.

Simulated Trade Practice Tips:

<u>Ultimately you will perform as you practice</u>, and you can never get enough practice in mastering your craft. There are no limits to this gig, whether you're new or a longtimer, always something new to learn and improve.

Here's a simple mental checklist before you enter an MK Strategy Supply and Demand trade:

- Why is this a good entry beyond ZRCE?
- Where is my exit, both take-profit(s) and stop loss?
- Should I take this play or wait for a better one?
- Everything is solid, I will enter this trade <u>without reservation or hesitation</u>.

Can you consistently be right for three minutes/candles?

Always remember, the historic S&P average annual return is only six to eight percent, so anything at or above that is doing just fine. Even small amounts of profit really add up when trading larger contract sizes (e.g. $10 x 100 contracts = $1,000). Just rinse and repeat off major zones and you'll make good money.

Feeling foggy? Good, brain science says that mental fatigue indicates you're absorbing the information.

We've reached the end with but one final question for you to answer turning the page in your life.......

10

What's Next?

Congratulations on your new beginning!

Now what? You're in a race against yourself to become experienced. There are no shortcuts practicing and learning from others to increase your proficiency performing this new technical skill repeatedly and successfully.

Watch the one-hour webinar at MauriceKenny.com as I demonstrate how to recognize and draw zones, then start practicing! I also mention different scenarios you must prepare to handle (e.g. upward/downward trending, choppy).

Finally, I'm going to divulge THE TOP SECRET about the MK Strategy you've turned every page to discover. Ready? Here is the single truth hidden in plain sight: there is absolutely no secret sauce. Ta-dah! Worth the wait, huh? :)

You just finished reading all the basics you truly need. I detailed over these ten, short chapters enough for you to become a full-time day trader <u>IF you maintain mental discipline, follow your rules trading</u> <u>like an emotionless sniper and don't overcomplicate.</u>

However, very few will because we're human. Maybe YOU are the exception? I doubt because others before you read and applied this book, made good money, lost it all and THEN contacted me for coaching. Why? How did that happen?

Even the inventor of golf shanked shots. And playing golf, tennis, music and many other pursuits are similar to trading in the battle against oneself. With each you can learn the technical skills by reading, watching videos and practicing to your heart's content, but mentoring takes your game to another level because of two things, <u>experienced guidance and accountability</u>, neither of which you can do yourself. Sure you can teach yourself guitar, but will you be worth a lick? Even golf and tennis touring pros have coaches. Why should trading be different? I promise it isn't. We each learn from others in all aspects of life, either what to do or NOT do!

Some of you might be thinking, "Nah, I'll learn by myself through experience" and to you I say, yes indeed you will without a doubt, and your account balance will tell the tale of how you're doing. For all of us the Market is ultimately our teacher and the hard lessons learned hit you in the wallet aside from instances of dumb luck. Maybe you're really lucky? If true, why did you open this book?

Everyone gains experience over time but the choice you must make right now is whether to learn a complex skill sooner or later, totally on your own the difficult way, or invest in yourself and coaching to learn from the mistakes of others. You're still going to make your own mistakes even with coaching, but those will be fewer than making ALL the mistakes anew, and at least the course corrections will be guided and not simply random, fingers crossed, hoping and praying. If you don't have a system, then NO SYSTEM (pure guessing) is your system!

PROPER practice is critical to achieving success sooner than later. Just like in golf, tennis, shooting hoops, pitching, art and music, you can practice for hundreds of hours but also ingrain bad habits by not doing so properly. The misconception about expertise over 10,000 hours of practice is the necessity it must be correct, not simply accumulating hours. Practice doesn't make perfect, perfect practice does.

So if I've convinced you to explore coaching, watch the webinar first, then book a call to learn more about our program and whether we'll be a fit. We don't accept everyone because life is too short to deal with the annoying or know-it-alls.

If you're still unsure, watch hundreds of our students describe their experiences at MauriceKenny.com/Success-Stories.

"Trading this simple system I've made more money in such a relatively short amount of time that I'm mad at myself for not discovering sooner! But more valuable to me is the time freedom and being able to quit my thankless job. Thank you Maurice, my family thanks you too!" —Lori D.

Thank you for gifting me your minutes reading this book. I wish you good health, wealth and success living the life you dream and deserve!

BEFORE YOU CONTINUE READING

As my gift to you, here's access to my free one-hour webinar that will teach you my strategy that I use for day trading.

Don't have time to read the book? Scan the QR code below or go to the URL to learn about my strategy.

 Use your phone's camera to scan the QR code
OR
https://mauricekenny790.lpages.co/webinar-intro/

Made in the USA
Las Vegas, NV
03 December 2022

60052392R00076